The
NATURAL HISTORY
of
NEW YORK

Written by Stan Freeman
Illustrated by Mike Nasuti

Barn owl

Butter and eggs

Monarch butterfly

White-tailed deer

Hampshire House Publishing Co.

CONTENTS

American toad

Raccoon

Garter snake

Red-tailed hawk

View from Mount Van Hoevenberg in North Elba in the Adirondack Mountains

A little more than a century ago, America was not a land where the deer and the antelope played or the buffalo roamed. Populations of these animals and others had been reduced to the point that the survival of many species was very much in doubt.

Similarly, parts of the Northeast were nearly barren of many species of wildlife that had lived here for thousands of years, including black bears, moose, beavers and bald eagles.

The cutting of forests, plowing of meadows, damming of rivers and unrestricted hunting had taken their toll on wildlife.

To halt the decline in animal populations, laws that regulated hunting were established in many states in the early 1900s. This worked well for some animals, such as black bears and white-tailed deer, which gradually returned on their own to areas they had once inhabited.

In the case of animals that did not return on their own, wildlife biologists tried to raise them on game farms for release into the wild, or they captured wild animals in other states for release locally.

However, it was not enough to return these once-native animals to their historic territories. Their habitats – the land and water – also had to be restored. Loss of habitat is the primary reason most species of plants and

Bald eagle, threatened in New York

animals become rare or endangered. So thousands of acres of forests were bought to establish state and federal forests, parks and wildlife refuges, and rivers that had been fouled with sewage and trash were gradually cleaned up.

If animals were to be restored, they also had to be protected. In 1973, the federal Endangered Species Act was passed, making it a crime to hunt or otherwise harm many species of rare plants and animals. In addition, laws were passed in each state to protect plants or animals that were rare or endangered in that state.

State laws were also passed to protect wetland areas and water bodies, such as ponds, lakes, marshes and rivers. All living things depend on water for survival, and areas where land and water come together, such as the land surrounding a stream or river, are among the richest habitats for plants and animals.

Red-winged blackbirds and marsh wrens nest in the cattails of pond edges. Moose feed on vegetation found in swamps and marshes. Muskrats and river otters live much of their lives in water.

Today in New York, there are nearly 3,900 species of plants and animals considered native to the state. That does not even include the unknown number of invertebrate species – mainly insects.

New York's rare native species

Governments have set up a system to classify the health of populations of plants and animals. A species is considered endangered if it is on the verge of extinction in its natural range. It is threatened if it is likely to become endangered in the near future. It is on the federal endangered species list if it is endangered or threatened nationwide. It is on the state list if it is endangered or threatened in New York even though it may be more common in other states.

	Native species	Endangered state list/ federal list	Threatened state list/ federal list
Mammals	94	10/9	1/1
Birds[1]	375	10/3	10/1
Reptiles	39	7/3	5/3
Amphibians	33	2/0	0/0
Fish (inland only)	167	8/1	11/0
Invertebrates[2]	Not known	16/6	8/2
Plants	3,195	359/3	154/7
Total[3]	3,903	412/25	189/14

[1] Includes the bird species known to nest in New York as well as the non-nesting species that are regularly seen in the state
[2] Includes butterflies, moths, beetles, dragonflies, crustaceans, mussels, snails, worms and sponges
[3] Excludes invertebrates

Federal endangered species list includes these New York natives:	State endangered species list includes:
Shortnose sturgeon	All N.Y. species on the federal list
Roseate tern	Peregrine falcon
Blue whale	Tiger salamander
Indiana bat	Regal fritillary butterfly
Karner blue butterfly	Short-eared owl
Leatherback sea turtle	Mud turtle
Northeastern bulrush	Northern cricket frog

Great spangled fritillary, a native species

Black-eyed Susan, a native species

Invaders

Just like human beings, many plants can trace their roots to foreign soils. There are also animals that have ties to other places in America or abroad.

A range of weeds, wildflowers, trees, insects, fish, birds and other life forms were brought to the region over the years by gardeners, naturalists, cooks and sportsmen who admired them elsewhere and released them – or allowed them to escape – into the wild.

Others came as accidental hitchhikers on trucks, cars and airplanes and as stowaways on early sailing ships and ocean freighters. Still others arrived here on their own as part of the natural spread of their species into places where they could survive.

While the vast majority don't harm local ecosystems, a small percentage do. Called "invasives," these aggressive species invade and dominate the landscapes on which they alight, pushing out valued native species.

Some naturalists estimate that only about two-thirds of the plants found in the region were here before Europeans arrived. However, only two or three dozen of these late arrivals are considered seriously invasive.

For instance, purple loosestrife was introduced from Europe as a garden flower and eventually escaped into the wild. It has strikingly beautiful flowers, but it can quickly take over a wetland, such as a marsh, pushing out other native plant species, many of them important to nesting wetland birds.

European starlings, which were also natives of Europe, were released in Central Park in New York City in 1890 by a Shakespeare fan who wanted to introduce to America the birds mentioned in the immortal writer's plays. They have since spread from coast to coast and are reducing the populations of some other birds. Starlings nest in tree cavities, taking away nesting sites from other cavity-nesters such as bluebirds, northern flickers and tree swallows.

Oriental bittersweet is a fast-growing woody vine common to back yards that wraps around shrubs, trees and flowers, forming a thick tangle in which native species perish. In the fall it produces reddish-orange berries.

At least one species of harmful invader, the gypsy moth, was the result of a breeding experiment gone wrong. In 1869, hoping to start a silk business, a Massachusetts man tried to cross imported European gypsy moths with silk moths to create a more productive silkworm. But some of the gypsy moth caterpillars escaped.

Gypsy moths have now spread through most of the East. In some years, the gypsy moth caterpillars, which feed on tree leaves, damage more than a million acres of forests.

Oriental bittersweet, an invasive species introduced from Asia

European starling, an invasive species introduced from Europe

Purple loosestrife, an invasive species introduced from Europe

From northern cardinals and black-capped chickadees to great horned owls and bald eagles, the skies can seem nearly as populated with birds as the land is with people.

In fact, more populated. It's estimated there may be 20 times as many birds on earth as humans. Walk through any field or forest in summer and you can easily believe it.

Some 375 species of birds are native to New York, including nearly 245 that nest in the state. In all of North America, more than 800 species of birds have been reported. Worldwide, there are more than 9,000 species of birds.

While large forests in the state attract their share of birds that seek isolation from humans, such as scarlet tanagers and hermit thrushes, cities and suburbs are home to birds that can easily live around people, such as American goldfinches and mourning doves.

Cedar waxwing

much of their lives above the ground and in the air.

Even among birds, though, different species have evolved to have different features – variations in size, coloring, wing design or body shape. Because of these physical differences, some birds can find food in ways that others can't, or they can live and nest in places where others can't. As a result, more kinds of birds can survive than would be possible if all birds ate the same foods and lived and nested in the same places.

Birds born with a difference that gives them an advantage in finding food, such as a slightly longer beak, or an advantage in escaping predators, such as greater flying speed, are more likely to survive and have young. Therefore, their special features are more likely to be passed along to future generations.

Over millions of years, woodpeckers developed to have strong, sharp beaks, long tongues and sharp claws. They use their claws to grab onto the sides of trees, and they use their beaks to peck nest holes in trees and to dig beneath bark to find insects. They use their long tongues to grab the insects they find.

Nearly 150 million years ago, the first birds were appearing on earth. But they may have looked more like winged lizards than modern birds. Birds, like most creatures, have changed, or evolved, over millions of years to have specialized features that help them survive by giving them an advantage over other living things. The most important of these features is the ability to fly and to live

Hummingbirds developed to be very small (they are the smallest of all birds, sometimes weighing less than a

Songs and calls

The songs and calls of birds are their language. They use these sounds to tell other birds a territory is theirs, to attract a mate and to warn of danger. Their songs and calls may sound like this:

TUFTED TITMOUSE – "Peter! Peter! Peter!"
MOURNING DOVE – "Coo-ah, coo, coo, coo!"
GRAY CATBIRD – "Meow!"
OVENBIRD – "Teacher, teacher, teacher!"
GREAT HORNED OWL – "Who, who-who-who, who, who!"
EASTERN TOWHEE – "Drink your tea!"
BALTIMORE ORIOLE – "Tea too!"
WHITE-THROATED SPARROW – "Poor Sam Peabody, Peabody, Peabody!"
AMERICAN GOLDFINCH – "Potato chip!"
RED-WINGED BLACKBIRD – "Ok-a-lee!"
COMMON YELLOWTHROAT – "Witchity, witchity, witchity, witch!"
BLUE JAY – "Thief! Thief!"

American goldfinch

Tufted titmouse

Mourning dove

Great horned owl

Baltimore oriole

penny) and to have very strong wing muscles and long, thin beaks. They can beat their wings very rapidly, as fast as 75 times each second, to hover at flowers like bumble bees, and they use their long beaks like drinking straws to sip the nectar inside flowers.

Herons and egrets developed to have long, thin legs and long, sharp beaks. They use their legs to wade in the shallow water of lakes, streams and ponds. They can stand very still and wait for fish or tadpoles to pass by so that they can spear them with their beaks. To a fish, their thin legs may look like reeds.

In the Northeast, songbirds (a category that includes

Red-tailed hawks

most backyard birds) usually nest and lay their eggs from April to June. For smaller birds, like the tufted titmouse, white-breasted nuthatch and tree swallow, the eggs take about two weeks to hatch, and the young stay in the nest two to three weeks before they take their first flights.

For larger birds, such as great horned owls and red-tailed hawks, the eggs may take nearly four weeks to hatch, and the young may remain in the nest four to six weeks.

Birds in the wild have varying life spans. Harsh weather, accidents, disease and lack of food can take their toll. Most songbirds live only two to five years. However, some larger birds, such as mallards and great blue

Backyard birds of New York

Some birds will nest in residential areas. Shown for the birds below is: Nest construction – Average number of eggs per brood – Broods per season – Period during which eggs are laid – Time to hatching – Time to nestlings' first flights

Blue jay

A cup of rootlets, twigs, bark strips and leaves, usually in an evergreen tree 10 to 25 feet off the ground – Four or five eggs – One brood – April 15 to June 17 – About 17 days – About 19 days

Black-capped chickadee

A cavity in a standing dead tree lined with cottony fibers, fur, moss, hair, wool and feathers, usually 4 to 10 feet off the ground – Six to eight eggs – One brood – April 29 to July 15 – About 12 days – About 16 days

Ruby-throated hummingbird

A small cup of plant down, fibers and spider silk built in the fork of a drooping limb, usually 10 to 20 feet off the ground – Two eggs – One or two broods – May 21 to August 16 – About 16 days – About 19 days

American robin

A deep cup made of grasses and weed stalks and shaped with mud in the fork of a tree branch, in shrubs or on a window ledge, usually 5 to 15 feet off the ground – Three or four eggs – Two or three broods – March 23 to July 19 – About 12 days – About 15 days

Downy woodpecker

A cavity in a living or dead tree, usually 20 to 30 feet off the ground – Four or five eggs – One brood – May 6 to June 30 – About 12 days – About 21 days

House sparrow

A cavity lined with grasses, weeds and feathers in a tree, on a building, on a billboard or in a birdhouse, usually 10 to 50 feet off the ground – Four to six eggs – Two or three broods – March 23 to July 16 – About 12 days – About 16 days

Northern cardinal

A shallow cup of twigs, grasses, rootlets and vines in dense shrubs or thickets or in an evergreen tree, usually less than 10 feet off the ground – Three or four eggs – Two or three broods – April 10 to Sept. 9 – About 12 days – About 12 days herons, may live 20 years or more.

Birds are often specialists about food. Each species generally prefers one type of food. Canada geese like grass, eagles prefer fish, finches look for seeds and warblers like insects. However, most birds will eat more than one kind of food, and some will change their diet as the seasons change.

Feathers are a bird's clothing, keeping it warm in winter and giving it a colorful appearance. Robins may have 3,000 feathers. A tundra swan may have 25,000. However, most birds replace their feathers once or twice a year, a process called molting. The molt may take a month or more to complete.

Many birds, such as American goldfinches, grow their brightest feathers for the breeding season, when they are trying to attract mates. Then they grow duller colored feathers for the winter, which makes them less visible to predators.

Since it is the male's job to attract a female, in many species, including northern cardinals, American goldfinches and ruby-throated hummingbirds, the males have brighter feather coloring than the females. With plain coloring that often blends in with vegetation, females are more able to hide the nest and young.

Because northern winters can be harsh and food can

Range and migration routes for the scarlet tanager

Range during the breeding season

Migration routes

Range during winter

be scarce, most birds migrate in the fall to warmer regions in the southern United States and Central and South America. Then they return in the spring.

During the migration, many birds travel 200 to 300 miles a day. Some, like hawks and ducks, travel during daylight hours, but most smaller birds travel at night when they are less visible to predators.

Generally, the larger a bird, the faster it can fly. Finches and sparrows can reach top flying speeds of about 20 miles per hour, hawks can fly about 40 miles per hour and geese can fly about 60 miles per hour.

Peregrine falcons, which hunt from the air, may be capable of the fastest flying speeds, perhaps 120 to 200 miles per hour when they go into a dive.

CHECKLIST
Common birds of New York

Red-winged blackbird
8 in. from tip of beak to tip of tail
☐

Eastern bluebird
6 in.
☐

Northern cardinal
8 in.   M   F
☐

Black-capped chickadee
5 in.
☐

American crow
19 in.
☐

Mourning dove
12 in.
☐

Rock dove (pigeon)
13 in.
☐

House finch
6 in.
☐

Northern flicker
13 in.
☐

American goldfinch
5 in.   M   F
☐

Canada goose
38 in.
☐

Common grackle
12 in.
☐

Ring-billed gull
19 in.
☐

Great blue heron
48 in.
☐

M

F

Ruby-throated
hummingbird
3 in.

Blue jay
12 in.

Dark-eyed
junco
6 in.

Belted
kingfisher
13 in.

Mallard
23 in.

Northern
mockingbird
11 in.

White-breasted
nuthatch
6 in.

Baltimore
oriole
8 in.

American robin
10 in.

House sparrow
6 in.

Song sparrow
6 in.

White-throated
sparrow
7 in.

European
starling
8 in.

Tree
swallow
6 in.

Tufted
titmouse
6 in.

Cedar
waxwing
7 in.

Downy
woodpecker
6 in.

House
wren
5 in.

Raptors

Red-tailed
hawk
22 in.

American
kestrel
10 in.

Great horned
owl
22 in.

Screech
owl
9 in.

Bald eagle,
typical
wingspan,
80 in.

Peregrine
falcon
41 in.

American kestrel
23 in.

Broad-winged
hawk
33 in.

Turkey
vulture
72 in.

Northern
harrier
43 in.

Northern
goshawk
42 in.

Golden
eagle
84 in.

Sharp-shinned
hawk
23 in.

When a leaf falls in the forest, so the saying goes, an eagle will see it, a bear will smell it and a deer will hear it.

Gifted with extremely sharp hearing, white-tailed deer are perhaps the ultimate forest animals. Far from the delicate creatures many people think them, deer are tough and hardy survivors. They use their hearing to avoid the few predators they have, and they can live close to residential neighborhoods while rarely being seen.

White-tailed deer, with their large brown eyes, white tails and sleek, athletic forms, can be a striking sight. In the wild, they may live seven years or

White-tailed deer

more. The males (bucks) usually weigh 150 to 300 pounds, and females (does) may reach 100 to 200 pounds.

Bucks grow antlers each year and shed them in winter. If food is plentiful, a doe may breed when she is 6 months old and have a fawn around her first birthday in the spring. In later years, she may have one to three fawns each spring, which means deer populations can grow rapidly.

Deer prefer areas where there are forests mixed with clearings, wetlands, abandoned pastures or active farms. They are vegetarians, favoring the buds and twigs of young trees in the cold months, and grasses, fresh leaves and nuts, such as acorns, in the warm months.

Deer are swift runners, reaching speeds of 35 miles per hour.

In New York, there may be nearly a million white-tailed deer spread across the state, more than at any other time in history.

Area in red is range of species in New York.

2–3 in. long

White-tailed deer
may gather in dense stands of evergreens, called "deer yards," in severe winters with deep snow. Snow depths are usually less there, and deer can browse on the branches. The trees also give them protection from cold temperatures and blowing snow.

M O O S E

Moose disappeared from New York in the 1860s, eliminated mainly by hunting and the clearing of forests for farming.

But in the 1980s, these lumbering giants began to appear consistently in northeast New York, likely migrants from northern New England, where they had already made a strong comeback. There may now be 100 to 150 moose in the state, primarily in the Adirondacks.

As slow-moving and harmless as moose seem, though, they can pose a serious problem for people driving on highways. Moose are so large (they can weigh more than a half ton) that they usually feel no need to flee from danger, whether it's an approaching animal or an oncoming car. Moose often hold their ground, and that can result in

5–6 in. long

Moose

serious accidents when a car and a moose collide.

Moose can stand 6 feet at the shoulder, and their impressive weight sits atop long, spindly legs.

Moose are most likely to be seen near dawn and dusk when they are out foraging for food. They are most frequently seen in September and October, when males (bulls) are wandering in search of females (cows) during the breeding season. At that time of year, in areas where moose are found, you might hear the resounding bellows of bulls as they call to potential mates.

A bull's massive rack of antlers, which can be 5 feet across, is shed each year in winter. The antlers begin to grow in April and reach their full size by August. Moose are a type of deer, and as with all deer, the females do not grow antlers.

Moose keep to themselves much of the time, although several may gather in a feeding area. In winter, they feed mainly on twigs. In summer, they add aquatic plants, leaves and grasses to their diets.

Moose are
often found around swamps and lakes in summer, eating vegetation and submerging in the water to escape insects. In the wild, moose can live up to 20 years.

6–7 in. long

What is there about a bear that has such a dramatic effect on people? From affection for panda bears to fear of grizzly bears, human emotions run high at the sight of them. Indeed, to come face-to-face with a bear is perhaps the ultimate wildlife experience of the forest – and increasingly of the suburbs.

There may now be 5,000 to 6,000 black bears roaming upstate New York. Although primarily settled in the Adirondacks, the Catskills and on the Allegheny plateau, black bears travel widely and eventually visit nearly every upstate county.

With no major predators except humans, a bear can wander just about anywhere it wants, and many have discovered the food resources of residential areas, including bird feeders and trash cans.

Black bears have long suffered from a public relations problem created by the larger, more aggressive grizzly bears – which are not found anywhere near New York. The difference is that eastern black bears rarely attack human beings. They generally won't attack unless they are defending a cub or have been surprised.

Black bear

Black bears are not true hibernators. While a bear's heart rate drops dramatically during the winter dormancy, its temperature does not. In fact, only a few of New York's mammals are true hibernators, including woodchucks, jumping mice, chipmunks (although they will emerge from sleep to eat) and several species of bats.

Black bears, which can live 25 years or more, typically weigh 150 to 450 pounds, with males tending to weigh more than females. Bears eat little meat, focusing instead on plant matter that is available through the seasons, from skunk cabbage and grasses in the spring to apples and acorns in the fall. However, their taste for honey is well known.

Females give birth during their winter dormancy every other year, usually having two to four cubs.

COYOTES

2.5 in. long

Brush wolves. Sagebrush scavengers. Coyotes might make you think of western prairies and haunting howls on moonlit nights. But coyotes now reside near the hearts of many eastern cities, including New York City, prowling urban parks, passing themselves off to the casual observer as German shepherds or other bushy-tailed dogs.

Coyotes are recent arrivals to the Northeast, but they have already become common in the region. One theory is that western coyotes, which never were rare, moved north into Canada, bred with red wolves there, and produced a larger variety of coyote, which then moved south into New York, appearing in the state in the 1930s.

There may now be 20,000 to 30,000 coyotes in New York.

Eastern coyotes usually weigh 30 to 45 pounds, a bit more than western coyotes. They are grayish tan in color, but occasionally their coats can be blond, red or even charcoal black.

Strong swimmers, good jumpers (up to 15 feet) and swift runners (speeds of more than 30 miles per hour have been observed), eastern coyotes are also able hunters, with superior sight, smell and hearing.

Coyote

Coyotes, which are most active from dusk to dawn, are usually no threat to humans. They are expert scavengers, eating almost anything edible from the bottom of the food chain to the top – from berries, fruits and insects to mice, rabbits, white-tailed deer, and, yes, even the occasional cat. Eastern coyotes hunt alone, in mated pairs or in family groups.

Coyotes are famous for their howls in the night, a form of communication for them. They will even howl in response to sirens and train whistles.

The eastern coyote can look a lot like a German shepherd. However, coyotes are usually smaller and leaner. Also, a coyote's tail will usually be carried lower to the ground than that of a shepherd.

5 in. long

Beavers are nature's engineers, creating dams and lodges that are marvels of construction.

Virtually trapped out of existence in New York in Colonial times, beavers were reintroduced into the Adirondacks about 1900 and have thrived, thanks to a regulated trapping season.

From their protruding, orange-tinted, buck teeth to the end of their paddlelike tails, adult beavers are about 3 feet long, and they can weigh 30 to 65 pounds. They use their broad, flat tails as rudders when they swim, but they also use them to warn other beavers of danger by loudly slapping them on the water's surface.

Beavers use trees as their prime building material, and they also feed on the bark. Their favorite trees include poplars, birches, maples, willows and alders. They usually fell trees at night and are able to gnaw their way through a willow that is 5 inches in diameter in just a few minutes.

Beaver

Beavers dam streams to create ponds. They spend much of their lives in water, which protects them from predators. They begin by laying branches and twigs across a stream

Gnawed tree

that may be in a slight valley. Then they pack down this material with mud, extending the dam's width and height as they go.

Their trademark lodge can sit near the shore of a pond or right in the middle, surrounded by water.

In winter, beavers do not hibernate. They remain awake in the lodge, occasionally going out beneath the ice to retrieve tree branches they've stored in the water nearby for a meal. A beaver can stay submerged in water for up to 15 minutes.

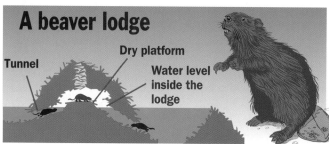

A beaver lodge

Tunnel

Dry platform

Water level inside the lodge

S Q U I R R E L S

Gray squirrel

Red squirrel

Northern flying squirrel

Gray squirrel track, 2.5 in. long

The squirrel is one of nature's bankers, wisely putting away resources for the future. Each fall, gray squirrels go about collecting nuts (their favorite food) and burying them one by one for the time when the snow falls and their sources of food disappear.

When winter arrives, they can find their stores, or caches, of acorns and other nuts beneath a foot of snow, not by remembering where they buried them but by smelling them.

Squirrels are rodents, as are chipmunks, woodchucks, beavers and mice. Most rodents hoard or store food to some extent.

In New York, eastern gray squirrels are the squirrels most commonly seen by people. With their quickness and ability to move acrobatically through the treetops, gray squirrels live easily around people and can thrive in residential areas with trees.

Red squirrels are common in many areas with evergreen trees, including residential neighborhoods. But northern and southern flying squirrels, which are also native to the state, are usually found in more remote forested areas.

Gray squirrels may have two litters each year, usually of two to four young per litter. One litter may be born in March and another in July or

Gray squirrel

Red squirrel

August. The spring litter is born in a tree den, which is a hollow cavity in a live tree also used during winter for shelter. The summer litter may be born in a large nest built high in a tree using leaves and sticks.

Although squirrels may stay in their dens for several days at a time when the weather is harsh in winter, they are active throughout the year.

Flying squirrels don't actually fly and they don't have wings. They spread open flaps of loose skin between their front and rear legs and glide through the air. Glides of up to 50 yards have been observed.

Northern flying squirrel

"Once bitten, twice shy" certainly applies to those who have encountered striped skunks. Sprayed just once with a skunk's unmistakable scent, and you will never want to repeat the experience.

Skunks have one of the more effective defenses against predators on the planet. Their scent spray, which can travel 15 feet in the air if the wind is right, is so strong it can temporarily blind a victim.

1.5 in. long

Their bold coloring – black with a white stripe running down their back – is meant to make the lesson that much more unforgettable. "If you see another animal that looks like this, stay clear," the distinctive colors seem to say.

Striped skunk

Skunks, which usually weigh 4 to 10 pounds, eat almost anything, including snails, small rodents, birds' eggs, fruit, grain, nuts, berries and garbage. Typically, they are nocturnal animals, and a sign one has been in your yard is shallow holes dug in the ground. A skunk was likely digging for grubs or worms during the night.

Skunks are usually active earlier in the spring than other mammals. They might spend the winter under a stump, in a stone wall, in an abandoned burrow or even under a house. But in mid-February the breeding season starts. Males may emerge from their dens and travel in search of females even when there is snow on the ground.

This is a time of year when wandering males often cross paths with dogs, coyotes and other non-hibernating species. For many people, the pungent odor that results is one of the first signs that spring is on the way.

Striped skunks usually do not spray without warning. Here's what to look for if you find yourself face-to-face with a skunk. When confronted, a skunk will usually face you, raise its tail, chatter its teeth and stomp the ground with its front feet. If this doesn't send you in retreat, it will then twist its rear end toward you while still facing you, and discharge its spray in your direction. There may be enough spray in reserve for four or five discharges. If the skunk scores a direct hit, don't even bother washing your clothes. Just throw them away.

FOXES

Red fox

Gray fox

Red fox track, 2 in. long

To see a red fox in the wild is memorable. True to its reputation, a fox is as sly as ... well, a fox. Very secretive, it can live close to residential areas but almost never be seen. It's also an impressive looking animal with its silky red fur and sharp features.

Red foxes are not animals primarily of the deep forest. They prefer farmland or forest edges. The suburbs, with its mix of fields and small wood lots, can also be an excellent habitat for them.

By contrast, gray foxes, which are less common in New York, usually live in forested or brushy areas.

Both red and gray foxes are smaller than most people expect, usually weighing just 7 to 14 pounds, about as much as a large house cat. They have varied diets, eating what animals and plants are available through the seasons, including rabbits, rodents, birds, insects, snakes, turtles, apples and berries.

Very often, foxes will not eat what they capture, especially if they are full. Instead, they will bury the prey for a later meal.

Vixens, or female foxes, bear their young in dens in late March or early April. They may have four to seven pups, which begin to spend time outside the den in early May. By late summer, the young will leave their parents' care permanently.

Unlike red foxes, gray foxes, which have sharp claws, will climb trees to reach potential prey, such as bird eggs. They will also scamper up a tree to escape danger. While a red fox den is nearly always underground, a gray fox will sometimes den off the ground in a hollow tree.

Red fox

Gray fox

Red foxes are active year-round. In winter, they hunt for small rodents, such as voles and mice, which move about in tunnels under the snow. A red fox's ears are very sensitive to low sounds, and it will sit on deep snow, listening for prey moving beneath it, then pounce, digging frantically, to capture the animal.

Yes, there are moose and bears and deer in the woods, but it is the small critters that really populate the great outdoors.

In a square mile of good habitat, there might be a few red foxes, a few dozen striped skunks, a few hundred eastern chipmunks and a few thousand short-tailed shrews. That's not to mention the brown bats, red squirrels, gray foxes, beavers, porcupines, cottontails, weasels, coyotes, woodchucks, otters, fishers, bobcats, muskrats, hares, voles, mice, minks and moles.

But if there are that many mammals out there, why do we see so few?

The reason is that many species are secretive and have habits that help them avoid predators (and human beings). For instance, many are nocturnal – active mainly at night. They sleep and rest in hidden places by day but then go out foraging for food once the sun goes down.

With so many animals sharing the same land, many have evolved to be specialists in where they live and what they eat so that they can survive despite the competition.

Muskrats, beavers and river otters spend much of their life in water. Shrews, moles and voles spend much of their life underground or under the cover of thick grasses or leaves. Squirrels and porcupines spend most of their time in trees. And bats fly.

Porcupines, rabbits and woodchucks are vegetarians. Moles eat worms and ground insects. Bats eat flying insects. Skunks, raccoons and opossums will eat almost anything that can be eaten, including garbage.

Even among mammals, though, there are predators and prey, roles that are often determined by size. The shrews, mice, voles and moles tend to be the prey, while

Raccoon

Woodchuck (groundhog)

the foxes, coyotes and bobcats are often the predators.

When approached by a predator, prey animals will use their specialized defenses. The opossum can act as if it's dead. The eastern cottontail can leap 15 feet. Snowshoe hares, which turn white in winter and blend with the snow, can run 30 miles per hour. Striped skunks can spray a fluid that smells terrible and can cause temporary blindness. Porcupines can protect themselves with their coat of sharp quills – as many as 30,000 needlelike spines.

In winter, many mammals either hibernate or become inactive in their dens or burrows. But some, such as coyotes and foxes, are active throughout the year.

It is not just the deep woods and rural meadows that are home to so many mammals. Even urban and suburban neighborhoods can be teeming with wild animals, and not just mammals. Many snakes, birds and insects also call this kind of habitat home.

Because many mammals, such as opossums and skunks, are nocturnal, you rarely see them in residential areas. But they're there. Ask any policeman who drives a cruiser on the midnight to dawn shift.

In fact, when an area is transformed from a rural to a residential landscape, some animals find life easier. They learn to adapt their diet to the new opportunities these neighborhoods can offer, such as bird feeders, vegetable gardens, trash cans, and healthy lawns and shrubs.

Many animals, such as squirrels, chipmunks and a variety of birds, live comfortably with people and are often in sight. Other animals, including garter snakes and woodchucks, live easily among people but prefer to stay out of sight as much as possible.

Opossum

Porcupine

Chipmunk

Eastern cottontail

Bobcat

Typical length is 27 to 38 in. – Typical weight is 12 to 35 lbs. – One or two litters per year of two to four young born in spring – Active before dusk to just after dawn in summer and also during the daytime in winter – Hunts deer in winter and small mammals, especially cottontails, and birds year-round – Dens in a rock crevice or hollow log – Active throughout the year

2 in. long

River otter

3 in. wide

35 to 54 in. – 12 to 20 lbs. – One litter per year of two to four young born March or April – Active mainly from dusk to after dawn, but can be active any time of day – Eats primarily fish, but also frogs, turtles and aquatic insects – Dens in a rock crevice, under a fallen tree, in an abandoned beaver lodge or muskrat house or in thickets beside water – Active throughout the year

Eastern cottontail

14 to 18 in. – 2 to 4 lbs. – Three to seven litters per year of three to six young – Most active dusk to just after dawn – Eats mainly plant matter, such as grasses and herbs, in summer, and bark, twigs and buds in winter – Finds shelter year-round in brush piles, stone walls or abandoned dens and burrows – Active year-round, although retreats to shelter during harsh winter weather

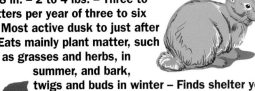

3–4 in. long

Chipmunk

1 in. long

8 to 10 in. – 2 to 5 oz. – One litter per year of three to five young born in April or May – Active all times of day – Eats mainly seeds, fruits, nuts and insects – Dens underground in a series of tunnels – Hibernates in winter, but may become active for short periods

Opossum

2.5 in. wide

26 to 35 in. – 5 to 9 lbs. – One or two litters per year usually of six to nine young, but sometimes as many as 20, born February to July – Active mainly at night – Eats nearly anything, including insects, fruits, nuts, carrion and garbage – Dens in an abandoned burrow, tree cavity, brush pile or thicket – Becomes less active in winter, but does not hibernate

Porcupine

3 in. long

24 to 30 in. – 8 to 20 lbs. – One litter per year of one young born April to June – Active mainly at night – A strict vegetarian, it eats grasses, twigs, buds and bark – Most den in winter in rocky fissures, hollow trees and logs or vacant buildings, such as sheds, but they may emerge to feed during the day – Active throughout the year

Raccoon

3.5 in. long

22 to 34 in. – 15 to 25 lbs. – One litter per year of three to seven young born April or May – Active mainly at night – Eats everything from small animals and birds to grains and garbage – Dens in a ground cavity, hollow tree, hollow log, pile of rubbish, attic or chimney – Spends winters in its den, but does not hibernate

Muskrat

19 to 25 in. – 1 to 4 lbs. – Two to four litters per year of three to eight young born April to September – Active mainly at night, but may be seen during the day – Eats mainly aquatic plants, such as cattails and pond weeds – Constructs a lodge of weeds on water or digs a den in a stream bank – Active throughout the year

2 in. long

Little brown bat

3 to 4 in. – .1 to .5 oz. – One litter per year of one young born mid-June to mid-July – Active mainly at night – Eats flying insects – Spends winters in a cave or abandoned mine, but female may nest in attics or barns to bear young – Hibernates in winter

Woodchuck

2 in. long

19 to 27 in. – 4 to 14 lbs. – One litter per year of four to six young born early April to mid-May – Active by day, especially in the early morning and late afternoon – Eats mainly plants, such as clover and grasses – Dens in a series of underground tunnels ending in a chamber with a grass nest – Hibernates in winter

Garter snakes may have 40 of them, opossums usually have about eight, catbirds often have four, and bats and porcupines have just one.

What are they? They're offspring. And different species of animals may have very different numbers of young when they become parents.

There are other differences as well in the reproductive habits of animals. Birds, butterflies and frogs lay eggs, but mammals, such as foxes, chipmunks and bears, have live young. Turtles may never meet their mothers, deer fawns may stay with their mothers nearly a year, and crows may stay together as a family composed of several generations.

But like most things that animals do, there is a purpose and a plan to the way they raise their families.

Somewhere in their development, species faced choices. To best ensure that your species survives, do you have a lot of young or just a few? Do you spend a lot of time taking care of the offspring or very little?

For instance, if a mother has lots of young each season, the chances are greater that some will survive to adulthood so they too can have families and keep the species alive. However, if she does have lots of young, she will have a harder time feeding them than if she has just a few babies. So which approach is best for species survival?

Animals do not consciously choose to use one approach or another. Essentially, life makes the decision for them. Let's say there is a species of animal in which litter size varies greatly. Some mothers have the biological trait – the genes – for having small litters, and some have the genes for large litters. But let's say that because of a permanent change in the availability of food, the young

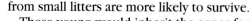

Red fox pup

Deer fawn

from small litters are more likely to survive.

These young would inherit the genes for small litters from their parents, and when they get to be parents, they will have small litters too. In not too many generations, most families of this species will be having small litters, and large litters might disappear completely.

If a species has lasted a long time on earth, chances are its method of reproduction has worked well. It is probably right for that species' situation.

For instance, birds need to be light to fly, and they need to eat a lot of food in comparison to their weight in order to have the energy to fly. They might have had a hard time surviving if they did not lay eggs. A mother bird might weigh too much to fly and feed if she were carrying her young inside her as they developed. She might also be more vulnerable to predators. So eggs that develop outside a mother's body are a good solution for birds.

Sometimes, though, different approaches to reproduction work just as well. Some snakes, such as garter snakes, have live young, while others, such as milk snakes, lay eggs. The fact that snakes using each method are common seems to say neither method has a clear advantage for them.

Spring is the time for offspring. Baby red foxes, woodchucks and river otters might be born just as spring starts. Mallards often lay eggs in April that hatch in May. Bobcats, skunks and chipmunks might have their young in May. Most songbirds, such as northern cardinals and tree sparrows, lay their eggs in May and June. Deer and little brown bats might be born in June.

For animals that are cared for by their parents, how long they remain in the nest or den varies by species. But as a general rule, the larger an animal is, the longer it will stay in the care of its parents.

Bluebird bringing food to the nest

Bobcat kitten

The birds and the bees: Family planning in the animal kingdom

PAINTED TURTLE – Up to 11 eggs are laid in a hole dug on land in late spring, then the mother leaves the nest permanently. The eggs take about 75 days to hatch, then the young find water on their own.

GREEN FROG – As many as 4,000 eggs are laid in jelly-like masses in water, typically in mid-spring. The eggs hatch in three to six days, and the young spend one or two years as tadpoles before changing into frogs.

HONEY BEE – The queen bee may lay 1,200 eggs a day and 200,000 eggs a season. An egg develops in a wax cell in the hive's brood area, hatching in about three days.

RED-TAILED HAWK – Typically, two or three eggs are laid in a stick nest built high in a tall tree. The eggs hatch in about a month. The young take first flights about 45 days later.

MEADOW VOLE – Also called field mice, these small mammals may have as many as 10 litters of live young a year, and there may be up to 10 young per litter. The young may spend only two weeks being fed by their mother before they are on their own.

GARDEN SPIDER – Hundreds of eggs are laid in a sac on a leaf, twig or a support in the fall. The mother dies when the weather turns cold and the spiderlings overwinter in the egg sac.

WHITE-TAILED DEER – Usually two fawns are born in late May or early June. They feed on their mother's milk for about three weeks, then they begin to browse on vegetation. Males may leave their mothers by the fall. Females may stay with them up to two years.

RACCOON – Typically, three to seven young are born in a hollow tree in April or May. The young, which have the characteristic mask of raccoons soon after birth, venture from the den in about seven weeks to run and climb.

HUMPBACK WHALE – One and sometimes two calves are born tail-first in warm tropical waters in the winter or early spring after a gestation period of about a year. A newborn quickly swims to the surface to get its first breath of air.

GARTER SNAKE – Females give birth to live young. The litter, delivered between July and September, may number 14 to 40 young. The newborns are immediately on their own.

Baby skunk

Catbirds in their nest

What do you do if you find a baby animal?

You're walking through a field and come across a baby fawn standing motionless and alone in the tall grass. You find a baby bird beneath a tree in your back yard and there's no sign of either parent nearby. You accidentally uncover a nest of baby rabbits in thick grass on the edge of a lawn. What do you do?

Wildlife officials like to say, "If you care, leave them there."

In the majority of cases, an animal that appears to be orphaned really isn't. The mother may have wandered off in search of food, or she may be close by, waiting for you to leave. However, it may be that a young animal is out on its own. In the first days that animals leave the nest or den, they learn valuable lessons about finding food and protecting themselves that they will never have the chance to learn if you take them in without a good reason.

If the baby animal is truly abandoned or if you see an animal, baby or adult, that is obviously injured, call a veterinarian, an animal control officer or a licensed wildlife rehabilitator. If it's in your back yard, keep pet cats and dogs away while you wait.

If you decide it is necessary and safe to handle the animal, wear thick gloves and put it in a box with air holes and material, such as leaves or grass, on the bottom so that the animal does not slide around. Handle it as little as possible and call a wildlife officer.

However, it's not true that a mother animal will reject a baby if it has been touched by a human. She will take it back.

Most important, if the animal seems agitated or aggressive, do not handle it. Mammals, such as raccoons, foxes, skunks and bats, can carry rabies, a dangerous disease that can be passed to humans through an infected animal's saliva.

*Milk
snake*

The sudden discovery of a snake sunning itself on the front walk or slithering through the garden is enough to startle almost anyone. These reptiles can awaken primitive fears in people.

But despite the impressive size of some native snakes of New York (the black rat snake can reach a length of up to 8 feet), the chance of encountering one that could truly do you harm is very small. Of the 17 species of snakes that are native to the state, only three are venomous – the timber rattlesnake, the eastern massasauga and the northern copperhead. They are usually found in remote spots in the state, places humans rarely inhabit, such as high on rocky mountainsides.

Snakes live everywhere in the state, from the coastal plains of Long Island to the high slopes of the Adirondacks. You're most likely to see a snake in the spring, when it is out of hibernation and basking in the sun. Snakes cannot easily adjust their body temperature in cold weather, so they warm up by sunbathing.

The snake you're most likely to see is the garter snake, the most common snake in the state. Many snakes, such as the black racer, lay eggs, but others, such as the garter snake, have live young.

The northern water snake is the next most common

Black rat snake

Ringneck snake

snake in the state. A harmless snake, it is frequently mistaken for the poisonous water moccasin, also called the cottonmouth. However, there are no water moccasins north of Virginia.

The damage from being bitten by a non-venomous snake is more psychological than physical. The wound is typically no more serious than being scratched by a thorn on a rosebush.

Smaller snakes usually search for insects, slugs, earthworms, frogs or toads for their meals. Larger snakes may also hunt small rodents and birds. All snakes swallow their prey whole, usually seizing the prey first with their jaws. However, a few snakes, including the black rat snake and milk snake, may wrap their body around the prey and squeeze it to make the kill.

Some snakes, such as the milk snake and black racer, will vibrate their tails as a display to scare away predators. People often mistake this for the rattle of a timber rattlesnake. But the rattlesnake has a very distinct rattle on it that when shaken sounds almost like a baby's rattle.

In winter, snakes in the Northeast hibernate in burrows or hollows or even in holes in the foundations of homes.

Most snakes are hatched or born in the summer, and they are left on their own to find food from the start. As snakes grow, they periodically shed their outer skin – like throwing away an old set of clothes – because they outgrow it. This is called shedding or molting.

New York's snakes
(Average length)

Worm snake
Redbelly snake
Brown snake
Ringneck snake
Smooth green snake
Short-headed garter snake
Eastern ribbon snake
Eastern hognose snake
Common garter snake
Queen snake
Milk snake
Eastern massasauga snake
Northern copperhead
Northern water snake
Timber rattlesnake
Black racer
Black rat snake

0 feet   1   2   3   4

Garter snake

Painted turtle, 4 to 10 in.

Box turtle, 4 to 8.5 in.

Even nature believes you don't fix what isn't broken. Despite being slower and more awkward than almost any other animal, turtles have changed remarkably little since they first appeared nearly 220 million years ago, well before most dinosaurs.

Their basic design – everything contained inside a hard shell – has worked very well for them, providing them excellent protection against predators. In fact, some turtles may live 100 years or more.

The chief threat to turtles is humans. Many turtles are disappearing from the wild because they are collected for the pet trade. Some species are vanishing because their nesting sites, the places where they go to lay eggs, have been developed for businesses and homes.

Like snakes, turtles are reptiles, which means they cannot warm their bodies from the inside the way humans and other mammals do. Instead, reptiles must take action to warm up. For instance, they can bask in the sun. On cool spring days or on summer mornings, you will often see turtles in ponds doing just this, as they sit on top of logs or rocks.

Turtles have no teeth. They use their hard bills to scissor apart their food. In water, they eat aquatic insects, fish, frogs and plants. On land, earthworms, snails, grasshoppers, fruits and berries are part of their diet.

A turtle's shell is both its mobile home and its protection. The top part of the shell, called the carapace, is attached to the turtle's backbone. The lower half of the shell is called the plastron. Despite what you see in cartoons, turtles cannot leave their shells.

The box turtle has a hinge on its plastron so that when it pulls in its head and legs to escape a predator the shell closes up, leaving almost no flesh visible.

Turtles have lungs but no gills. Some are able to breathe underwater by absorbing oxygen from the water through their exposed skin.

In winter, many turtles settle down into the mud at the bottom of ponds or rivers to hibernate. Land turtles, such as the box turtle, dig beneath soft dirt or decaying leaves to hibernate.

Snapping turtle 8 to 19 in.

Worldwide, there are nearly 250 species of turtles, including 20 that are native to New York.

The most common turtles found in the state, and the only two that can be found throughout the state, are the painted and snapping turtles.

The painted turtle lives almost anywhere there are ponds, lakes or slow-moving streams or rivers. Snapping turtles, which spend most of their time underwater, are rarely seen except during the breeding season.

Many New York turtles are found in only a few locations in the state. The yellowbelly slider and the green turtle have been seen only on Long Island. The eastern spiny softshell turtle has been found only in western New York.

In fact, eight of the state's 20 turtles, including the mud turtle, bog turtle and leatherback sea turtle, are either endangered or threatened in the state.

Turtles all lay eggs in the ground. Even a turtle that spends nearly all its life in water comes onto land to bury up to several dozen eggs in a shallow hole it digs in late spring or early summer. Most turtle eggs hatch from August to October, with a peak in September.

Musk turtle, 3 to 5.5 in.

Wood turtle, 5 to 9 in.

If there were an animal Olympics, frogs would certainly be competitors in the standing long jump. Some can leap 20 times their body length.

Lots of animals are specialists physically. They have a feature that gives them an advantage over other animals in finding food or defending themselves, and that's why their species has survived over the centuries. Frogs use their tremendous jumping ability both to escape predators and to pounce on a meal.

Bullfrog, 3 to 8 in.

Frogs are amphibians, which means they spend part of their lives in water and part on land. They are also among the animals that undergo metamorphosis, which means a "change in form." As young tadpoles (also called polliwogs), they live in water and look like small fish with large rounded heads. They have gills, tails and no legs. But eventually they develop lungs and legs, they will lose their tails, and, as frogs, they will be able to live on land.

There may be nearly 4,000 species of frogs worldwide. (This includes toads, which technically are a kind of frog.) Some 14 species of frogs can be found in New York.

Most adult frogs have large hind legs for jumping, hind toes that are connected by webbing, no claws and tiny teeth (if they have any at all).

Some, such as the eastern spadefoot, are rare enough in the state that you will probably never come across one in your lifetime. But others, like bullfrogs and green

Frog or toad?

You can usually tell the two apart by the texture of their skins. Frogs tend to have smoother skin, and they spend a lot of time in and around water. Toads have rougher, warty skin and usually can be found on land.

frogs, are so common that you can't miss them. In spring or summer, walk down to the edge of any pond and you may see a green frog sitting very still on the bank or a bullfrog peering at you from the water, its two bulging eyes and a bit of its head breaking the pond's surface.

Spend any time around a pond and you'll also hear frogs calling, or chorusing, especially during breeding season, which usually peaks in the spring. Male frogs are the ones making all the noise. They call to attract females and to announce that a territory is theirs.

A frog enhances its call by using a loose pouch of skin at its throat that it can fill with air. When it calls, the sound that is produced in its larynx enters this air-filled chamber and reverberates, like an echo in a cave, becoming even more intense. A male frog might repeat its call thousands of times in one night.

Nearly all frogs lay jellylike eggs in water, often thousands of eggs at a time, which eventually hatch to become tadpoles.

In winter, frogs become inactive, settling down into the mud at the bottom of ponds or taking refuge under piles of dead leaves or in underground tunnels on land. In the coldest weather, some even partially freeze but are still able to thaw out and resume their lives in the spring.

Most frogs eat insects, such as ants and flies, as well as worms and snails. However, the bullfrog, which is the largest native New York frog, will eat fish, snakes, mice and even small birds or newly hatched turtles that venture too close.

American toad, 2 to 4.5 in.

Leopard frog, 2 to 5 in.

Green frog, 2 to 4 in.

Many of New York's frogs are found statewide, including bullfrogs, green frogs, wood frogs, American toads and spring peepers.

However, some rarer frogs are only found in certain regions. Mink frogs are seen mainly in the Adirondacks. Western chorus frogs occur primarily near the Great Lakes and in the St. Lawrence River Valley. Fowler's toads are seen mainly on Long Island and in the Hudson River Valley.

In recent years, biologists have noticed a growing problem among amphibians. Many have deformities, such as missing or extra limbs. In addition, populations of frogs in some places in the world are declining dramatically.

Researchers are not sure what the reason is for the troubling problem. A leading theory is that it may be due to parasites, such as flatworms, that invade developing amphibians.

The problem could also be due to pesticides in the water or the thinning of the atmosphere's ozone layer, which allows more ultraviolet light to reach the earth's surface and the fragile eggs of amphibians.

Humans versus animals

Human world record as of May 2002 compared with the observed performance of animals in the wild

Marathon
(26 miles, 385 yards)
Human: 2 hr., 5 min., 42 sec.
Pronghorn antelope: About 45 min.

High jump
Human: 8 ft., .5 in.
Killer whale: 15 to 17 ft.

Speed on land
(100 meter dash)
Human: 9.79 sec.
Cheetah: About 3.2 sec.

Speed in water
(100 meter freestyle)
Human: 47.84 sec.
Sailfish: About 3.3 sec.

Long jump
Human: 29 ft., 4.75 in.
Snow leopard: About 50 ft.

Vernal pools

On the first warm night that follows a heavy rain each spring, an amazing event occurs. Certain frogs and salamanders that are rarely seen at any other time of the year come out of hiding and begin moving through the woods in great numbers.

Crowds of frogs. Parades of salamanders.

They are migrating to pools of water left by melted snow on forest floors. They may cross roads, hike up hills and climb over rocks and fallen trees in their determination to reach these temporary patches of water, called vernal pools.

Because the water dries up in the heat of summer, these pools do not contain fish. That makes them ideal breeding ponds for these amphibians, since there will be no predatory fish in the water to eat their eggs or their developing young.

Wood frog, 1.5 to 3.5 in.

In New York, wood frogs make this trek, as do spotted, blue-spotted, marbled, red and Jefferson salamanders.

During March and April, you can locate some of these breeding pools by the sounds that come from them at night. Wood frogs will chorus, making a noise that resembles ducks quacking.

Once these amphibians reach their vernal pool, which they may return to year after year, they must court, breed and lay their eggs in a short period of time.

They are active by day, but most of the activity is at night, especially among the salamanders.

If you can locate a vernal pool in the spring, take a flashlight, shine it on the water after dark, and you might see dozens of these creatures swimming about.

Spotted salamander 6 to 10 in.

What monarch butterflies do each fall is just about the definition of impossible.

Each September, tens of millions of these regal orange and black butterflies leave their summer breeding grounds in the United States and Canada and flutter off toward their winter home on a few remote mountainsides in Central Mexico. They return to the very same trees that previous generations returned to in their southern migrations for perhaps thousands of years. Then, in March, they may lift off nearly all at once, forming great clouds of butterflies that fill the sky as they return north.

Monarch

But the astounding thing is that adult monarchs may live less than one month in summer. That means that none of the monarchs that leave Mexico in the spring are among those that return in the fall. Instead, it is their great-great-grandchildren that will somehow find their way back to those few Mexican mountainsides with no one in their band of migrating monarchs ever having been there.

How do they do it? Is it in their genes? Are they guided by the earth's magnetic field? Or is it just one of the mysteries of animal instincts?

Butterflies, like all insects, go through a metamorphosis, or a change in appearance, except that for butterflies it is one of the most striking changes.

Butterflies have four stages to their lives – egg, larva (also called a caterpillar), pupa (also called a chrysalis), then adult butterfly.

In the pupa stage, the caterpillar forms a shell-like covering around itself and hangs by thin threads from a twig or leaf. Inside, the caterpillar can change from a fairly clumsy, slow-moving and perhaps, to some, even ugly creature into what can be a beautiful, brilliantly colored butterfly, carrying the colors of the rainbow on its fragile wings.

Butterflies feed on nectar, a sweet liquid produced deep inside flowers. To do this, a butterfly uses its proboscis, a long narrow tube like a drinking straw that can be almost as long as its body. When it's not in use, the proboscis is kept curled up where you would expect the butterfly's mouth to be.

Butterflies need the heat of the sun to warm their bodies, so they tend to be most active during the middle of the day. At night, they rest.

Butterflies have three body parts – the head, the thorax or middle section, and the abdomen. They have six legs, and four wings – a pair each of front and back wings.

The colors on their wings are created by tiny colored scales that fit together like tiles in a mosaic.

Most adult butterflies live only two to four weeks, surviving mainly to mate and produce eggs. The female searches for certain kinds of plants on which to lay her eggs, since they are food plants for the young caterpillars. Monarchs choose milkweed. White admirals like wild cherry and poplar leaves. Tiger swallowtails prefer black cherry leaves.

There are about 145 species of butterflies that breed in New York. There are nearly 30 other species that are occasionally seen in the state, often arriving on the winds of a storm or on a strong breeze from the Midwest or South.

Butterfly or moth?

There are lots of differences. Butterflies usually fly during the day. Moths usually fly at night. Butterflies tend to rest with their wings folded up over their heads or stretched flat to each side. Moths often lay their wings flat and behind them while resting. The antennae of butterflies are thin and end in a knob. Those of moths do not end in a knob and are often feathery. Butterflies usually have bolder and brighter colors than moths, although there are some strikingly colored moths.

Moth

Butterfly

Eastern tiger swallowtail

Eastern black swallowtail

CHECKLIST
Common butterflies of New York

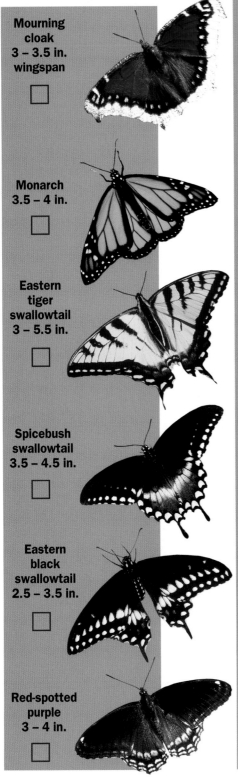

Mourning cloak
3 – 3.5 in. wingspan
☐

Monarch
3.5 – 4 in.
☐

Eastern tiger swallowtail
3 – 5.5 in.
☐

Spicebush swallowtail
3.5 – 4.5 in.
☐

Eastern black swallowtail
2.5 – 3.5 in.
☐

Red-spotted purple
3 – 4 in.
☐

Red admiral
2 – 2.5 in.
☐

Great spangled fritillary
2 – 3 in.
☐

Baltimore checkerspot
1.5 – 2.5 in.
☐

Pearl crescent
1 – 1.5 in.
☐

Eastern comma
1.5 – 2 in.
☐

American copper
About 1 in.
☐

Painted lady
2 – 2.5 in.
☐

Spring azure
About 1 in.
☐

Cabbage white
1.5 – 2 in.
☐

Clouded sulphur
1.5 – 2 in.
☐

Silver-spotted skipper
1.5 – 2.5 in.
☐

Common ringlet
1 – 2 in.
☐

Little wood satyr
1.5 – 2 in.
☐

Banded hairstreak
1 – 1.5 in.
☐

At most family reunions, get all the relatives together in one room and you can usually see a resemblance.

But put a caterpillar and a butterfly side by side, or a tadpole and a frog next to each other, and not only is there no family resemblance, there's not even a species resemblance. Why does this happen?

Nature devised this dramatic change in appearance, this metamorphosis, as a way of ensuring that these species would survive.

Many features of plants and animals – the long legs of a great blue heron, the rich color of a rose, the sharp beak of a hawk – evolved or developed because they give a species a better chance for survival. They are features that give it an edge in finding food or in reproducing or in protecting itself from predators.

Metamorphosis is no different. Species that change form (and all amphibians and nearly all insects go through some type of metamorphosis) can occupy two very different places in the ecosystem. The young may eat one kind of food, go through metamorphosis, and then eat a different kind of food as adults. That means there is more food available for the entire species, increasing its chance for survival.

Tadpoles are vegetarians, but adult bullfrogs eat almost anything, from plants to small birds. Most caterpillars feed

Bullfrog top, green frog below

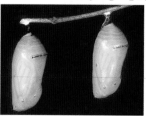

Monarch pupae

Monarch caterpillar

on leaves, but adult butterflies sip the rich nectar they find in flowers.

Having different forms at different stages of life can help in other ways as well. Caterpillars do almost nothing but eat and grow, and they are well-designed to do just that. They are able to avoid predators to some extent because most can blend into vegetation. They are also able to blend into their environment as pupae, the stage in which they are surrounded by mummylike coverings and undergo the changes that make them adult butterflies. Then, in the butterfly stage, they can fly to new areas to lay eggs and spread their species.

The changes tadpoles and caterpillars go through during metamorphosis are striking. Bullfrog tadpoles, which will be going from a life spent entirely in water to a life on land and in water, have to develop limbs and lungs during the change, and their tails have to be reabsorbed into their bodies.

Caterpillars, during the pupa stage, have to lose their many legs as well as develop wings and sex organs. They will also develop new mouth parts to draw nectar from flowers as adult butterflies.

For frogs, the metamorphosis usually lasts from several days to a few weeks. For butterflies, it may last from a few days to several months.

Monarch metamorphosis

In about 10 days, the adult butterfly emerges from the pupa, unfolds its wings, which slowly harden, then it flies away.

In the pupa stage, wings develop and the mouth parts change from chewing parts to sucking parts so that the adult butterfly can sip flower nectar.

Eggs are laid by female monarchs on the undersides of the leaves of milkweed plants. Each larva, or caterpillar, will eat its way out of its egg within a week and then begin to feed on the milkweed.

For the next two to three weeks, the caterpillar will feed and grow, shedding its skin every so often, a process called molting.

The caterpillar attaches itself by a silk thread and tiny hooks on its abdomen to a plant stalk and then sheds its skin one last time to reveal the pupa beneath.

Bullfrog metamorphosis

Within an egg, the embryonic cell divides within the first half day, and at four days, the developing tadpole has a tail bud and some muscle movement.

During reproduction, the male clasps the female, and she lays thousands of eggs in water. He then fertilizes the eggs with his sperm.

The egg hatches in water in about six days, and the tadpole clings to plants underwater. Within a day, it will begin to feed on algae.

A bullfrog spends about two years as a tadpole.

When the metamorphosis starts, hind legs begin to appear, and the gill system is gradually replaced by a lung system.

The frog is a mature adult in about three years. In New York, adult bullfrogs can weigh 4 pounds.

Within two weeks, the metamorphosis is usually complete. With its lungs, a frog can breathe air.

Long Island Sound as seen from East Marion in Suffolk County

What insects lack in size they make up for in numbers. More than 750,000 species of insects have been identified in the world. That's more than the number of all the other species of animals combined. And it may be only a fraction of all the insect species that actually exist on earth.

Bumble bee, .7 in.

Honey bee, .5 in.

common. They have six legs, three body sections and antennae. Spiders, with their eight legs, are not true insects.

Most insects can hear, taste, touch, smell and see, but many of them do these things in very different ways than humans. Crickets hear with their knees. Flies taste with their feet. Some moths and beetles smell with their antennae.

Despite their small size and short lives (some mosquitoes are lucky to live two weeks), insects are highly successful creatures. They have been able to thrive in almost every kind of habitat in almost every region of the world.

In fact, their short lives help to make them so successful. Insects reproduce quickly and in great numbers. So if there is any change in their surroundings – for instance, if the temperature warms dramatically – the chances are good that they will produce some young from the thousands of eggs they might lay (some termites lay 30,000 eggs a day) that have the right combination of genes to overcome the warmer weather. Some of those young will survive, reproduce more young with similar genes, and soon the local population will have adapted to the warmer climate and be thriving again.

Species that take a relatively long time to reproduce, such as some birds, which may have just two or three young a season, would not be able to adapt to dramatic changes in their habitat so quickly. Such changes might completely wipe out their local population.

All insects have certain things in

Most insects have two main eyes and two or three smaller, simpler eyes. The main eyes are sometimes made up of thousands of individual lenses, each of which produces an image.

Human eyes have one lens each, so the human brain has to interpret only the two images that its eyes send it. But a dragonfly's eyes may have 28,000 lenses each, which means its tiny brain has to interpret that many images in order to understand what it is seeing.

Nearly every insect goes through metamorphosis, a change in appearance marking a new stage of its life. Most insects look different as adults than as young emerging from eggs. Many are flightless when young but have wings as adults.

If you think the wings of a ruby-throated hummingbird move very fast, one species of midge, a tiny insect that is also known as a "no-see-um," beats its wings almost 1,000 times a second. That's nearly 13 times faster than the hummingbird beats its wings.

Bee or wasp?

Both can sting if bothered, but bees tend to have hairy bodies while wasps usually do not. Also, many bees, such as bumble bees and honey bees, have on their hind legs "pollen baskets" made of stiff hairs, where they carry the pollen they collect on their visits to flowers. Wasps do not have them. Hornets and yellow jackets are kinds of wasps.

Bumble bee   **Paper wasp**

Widow skimmer, 2 in.

Cecropia caterpillar, 4 in.

True katydid, 2 in.

Praying mantis, 3.5 in.

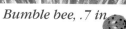

Fireflies

Also called lightning bugs, these beetles produce light in the tips of their abdomens by combining chemicals they produce and store in their bodies. Their blinking in summer is part of their mating process. Males fly about, flashing their lights to attract females that sit on leaves and branches.

There are nearly 200 species of fireflies in North America, and each has its own pattern of flashes to help males and females of the same species identify each other.

In the Northeast, the male of one of the most common fireflies *(Photinus pyralis)* flashes in low flight over grass about every six seconds, creating a yellowish "J" that lasts about half a second as he lifts into the air. The female, who sits on vegetation nearby, responds about two seconds later with a half-second flash of her own, an invitation for him to approach.

Grasshoppers and crickets

The "songs" of grasshoppers, like those of crickets, are the music of summer nights. However, these insects don't sing the way humans do. Grasshoppers rub a rough part of a back leg against their wings to create their music, and crickets rub their wings together. They make these noises to attract females and to chase away other males.

Ladybugs

Probably the best known of beetles, ladybugs are among the most valuable beetles to humans. They generally do not eat plants, but they do eat small insects that eat plants, which makes them important to farmers. In this region, you might see ladybugs with as few as zero spots or with as many as 19.

Ants

Like bees and other social insects, ants live in organized societies in which the members work together to keep the colony functioning. In all ant colonies, one queen ant is responsible for laying the eggs and producing the young.

Black carpenter ants, which are about a half-inch long, build their nests in dead wood, creating a series of tunnels and rooms. Unlike termites, they do not eat wood. They only tunnel into it.

Little black ants, which may be one-fourth the size of carpenter ants, usually build their nest underground, forming a little mound at the opening.

June bugs

Also called May beetles, June bugs are often seen buzzing around porch lights, or they are heard crashing into windows and screens at night. Unfortunately for them, they are attracted to electric lights. They are harmless to humans, though. As adults, they feed on the leaves of many common trees.

Mosquitoes

It is only the female mosquito that will bite you. The males feed mainly on flower nectar and fruit juices. The females need a meal of blood before laying eggs. Mosquitoes are most active at dawn, at dusk and at night. They hatch from eggs that develop in water, such as rainwater that collects in roadside ditches or in discarded tires.

House flies

Unwelcome guests at a picnic and a noisy distraction when they get inside a home or apartment, house flies live short lives and reproduce quickly. But they do not bite.

Their eggs can hatch in just a day, and the larvae can grow to adulthood in a week. A house fly may be hatched, mature, reproduce and die in the space of just a month, which means several generations of house flies can emerge during one summer.

Honey bees

Honey bees live in ordered communities in which each bee has a job. A honey beehive may have 50,000 members. There is only one queen bee, and her job is to lay eggs. There may be 1,000 male drones in the hive, and their only job is to mate with the queen, although only one will be successful. The rest of the hive's members are female worker bees, and they can have many jobs during their brief lives. Here is the typical life cycle of one worker bee in summer.

DAY 1–3
The egg is laid and develops within a wax cell.

DAY 4–20
The larva emerges from the egg, feeds, and then develops into an adult worker bee.

DAY 21–23
The worker bee's first job is as a cleaner, readying the brood cells for the next batch of eggs.

DAY 24–27
It becomes a nurse, feeding the older larvae.

DAY 28–34
It continues as a nurse, feeding the younger larvae and the queen.

DAY 35–41
It becomes a food collector, searching outside the hive for pollen, a rich source of protein.

DAY 42–death
It continues as a food collector, searching outside the hive for nectar, a rich source of energy.

At different times, the worker bee may also be a fanner (beating its wings to keep the hive cool), an undertaker (removing the bodies of dead bees from the hive), a soldier (guarding the hive's entrance) or a builder (creating wax to add to the hive walls).

Eastern pondhawk, 2 in. body length

Halloween pennant, 1.5 in.

As if the passion of the public for boldly colored winged creatures can't be satisfied by birds and butterflies alone, dragonflies are now attracting their faithful followers.

And why not? They are elegant creatures, capable of mid-air acrobatics that few birds can match. They are also the friends of anyone who doesn't like mosquitoes. The reason dragonflies spend so much time hovering over ponds is that they are hunting mosquitoes, which are their primary food.

Worldwide, there are more than 5,000 species of dragonflies and damselflies, including nearly 450 species that have been seen in North America.

Like birds, dragonflies fly and lay eggs. Some, like the green darner, even migrate to warmer regions when the weather turns cold.

But like butterflies and other insects, they go through metamorphosis, changing appearance before entering the adult stage of their lives.

The eggs of dragonflies, which are

Twelve-spotted skimmer, 2 in.

laid in or near water, may hatch in five to 10 days. The larvae that emerge then begin the process of eating and growing. They consume everything from mosquito larvae to tiny fish, capturing their prey with a unique lower lip that has its own claw. The lip can shoot out to almost a third of a larva's body length to grab a meal.

Larvae that hatch in the summer often spend the winter growing before transforming into adult dragonflies the following spring.

Unlike many insects, dragonflies go directly from water-bound larvae to flying adults without a pupal stage. When it is ready to make the change, the larva climbs out of the water, takes hold of a reed or twig, and sheds its skin, allowing the soft, folded wings beneath to slowly fill with blood and harden. After several hours, the adult dragonfly takes to the air.

Many dragonflies live only about a month as adults, time enough to mate (usually accomplished in mid-air) and to lay eggs before dying.

Dragonfly or damselfly?

Dragonflies and damselflies are both found flying over ponds, swamps and other still water bodies. You can tell the two apart by how they hold their wings when at rest. A dragonfly will stretch them out from side to side. Damselflies, which have thin, needle-like bodies, rest with their wings folded in back of them close to their sides. Contrary to myth, neither dragonflies nor damselflies bite humans.

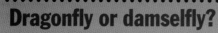

Dragonfly   **Damselfly**

Big bugs

Insects can be small but they can also be large. Here are a few of the larger New York varieties shown at their actual size.

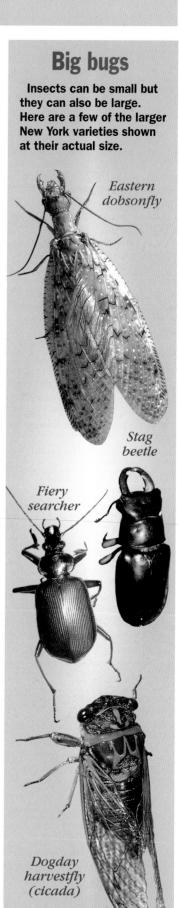

Eastern dobsonfly

Stag beetle

Fiery searcher

Dogday harvestfly (cicada)

What tangled webs they weave.

Worldwide, nearly 35,000 kinds of spiders have been identified, including nearly 600 species in New York.

You can tell a spider by its two body sections and eight legs. Most also have eight eyes.

Wolf spider, .8 in. body length

Shamrock spider, .4 in.

Many spiders are active only at night, and most are not very aggressive. Even those with the strongest venom will attack humans only as a defensive measure, preferring to retreat from battle whenever possible.

Because of the Northeast's chilly winters, most spiders found in New York live just one season, hatching in

Crab spider, .4 in.

the spring, breeding and laying eggs in the summer, and dying in the fall.

But a certain number manage to live through the winter. They may try to escape harsh weather by seeking refuge in the cozy interior of your home or apartment. A large house can be home to hundreds of spiders in winter, with the human residents barely aware of their presence.

Most spiders you are likely to encounter in New York would be too small to pose a threat. As a general rule, only those with a body over half an inch in length (not including legs) have fangs capable of penetrating human skin. But that does not mean they are dangerous. Even

larger spiders that bite are not usually a serious danger.

Just about all spiders are venomous. Even the smaller ones use venom to weaken or kill their prey. But only a few spiders have strong enough venom to cause harm to a human being.

The two most venomous spiders to be found in the United States are the brown recluse and the black widow.

The brown recluse is occasionally seen in New York. It sometimes arrives in the state as a hitchhiker on furniture or clothes brought from areas where it is more common, such as the Midwest. Its bite can have serious effects and must be treated quickly.

The black widow does occur on Long Island and Staten Island, but it is rare in upstate New York. The female is black with a red marking on its abdomen that is shaped like an hourglass.

The female black widow earned her name because soon after mating she eats the male. The males of most species of spiders are not treated so badly.

One of the largest spiders someone in New York might cross paths with is the wolf spider, often a resident of garden sheds, but sometimes an invader of homes. Its body can be more than an inch long. While painful, its bite usually does not have long-lasting effects.

Spider webs

The delicate webs that decorate dew-covered meadows or that float weightlessly in the corners of attic ceilings are actually wonders of engineering. Pound for pound, the silk in a spider web is stronger than steel.

Silk is created in a spider's abdomen, starting out as a sticky gel created in silk glands. It turns into a solid as it is pushed out of the body.

The final strand of silk may be less than a tenth the thickness of a human hair, but it can hold an astounding amount of weight.

As a comparison, a rope that is

an inch thick would have to support as many as 15 automobiles to have the same strength as some spider silk.

Aside from creating webs with their silk to snare passing flies and other prey, spiders use it as a safety line so that they can drop down from ceilings or branches. They also use silk to wrap their eggs for protection and to wrap prey for a later meal.

A spider may produce up to eight kinds of silk, each for a different use.

Same planet, different worlds. That's a good definition of ecosystems, the largely self-contained collections of plants, animals and ecological conditions that cover the landscape like different countries on a map.

A pond with bullfrogs, cattails and dragonflies can be near a forest where you might see hemlocks, wolf spiders and white-tailed deer. And just a stone's throw away can be a field where you might find monarch butterflies, oxeye daisies and meadow voles.

An ecosystem is a collection of living and non-living things, including plants, animals, ponds, streams, rocks and dirt, that all interact as a unit.

An ecosystem is created by a particular combination of water, land features, sunlight and temperature. Wherever you find that set of physical conditions in New York, you're likely to find the same general group of plants and animals, called an ecological community.

An ecosystem can include a stream or a pond, or it can include a combination of a stream and a pond. An ecosystem can include a meadow in a valley or a meadow on a mountainside.

An ecosystem can be as small as a single small pool of water left from melted snow on a forest floor in spring,

Ecozones of New York

In an ecozone, the same general physical conditions tend to prevail. Here are examples of ecological communities found in the state's different ecozones. Some communities may be found in all ecozones, and one ecozone may contain dozens of different communities.

1 St. Lawrence plains
Northern hardwood forest, pastureland, beech-maple mesic forest

12 Mohawk Valley
Rocky headwater stream, floodplain forest, flower/herb garden

11 Great Lakes plains
Inland salt pond, Great Lakes dunes, oak openings

10 Allegheny plateau
Oxbow lake, urban vacant lot, Appalachian oak-hickory forest

2 Champlain Valley
Silver maple-ash swamp, successional old field, cobble shore wet meadow

9 Triassic lowlands
Unpaved road/path, rocky summit grassland, oak-tulip tree forest

3 Adirondack highlands
Alpine meadow, spruce-northern hardwood forest, black spruce-tamarack bog

4 Taconic highlands
Vernal pool, Appalachian oak-pine forest, successional shrubland

5 Hudson Valley
Confined river, dwarf pine ridge, tidal river

6 Hudson highlands
Chestnut-oak forest, successional southern hardwood forest

7 Manhattan hills
Cliff community, mowed lawn with trees, serpentine barrens

8 Coastal lowlands
Pitch pine forest, sand beach, maritime dunes

or it can be as large as the whole forest, including the pool of water. Ecosystems are also found in cities. A vacant lot between two buildings may eventually become home to a variety of wildflowers, insects, birds and small mammals.

Ecosystems do not have barriers between them, though. They overlap and share resources. Insects, birds and other animals move between ecosystems.

If the conditions of a landscape determine the plants and animals that live on that landscape, then New York, with its spectacular range of conditions, should feature a specular range of ecological communities. And it does.

From the sandy coastal beaches on Long Island to the rocky peaks of the Adirondacks to the plains around the Great Lakes and St. Lawrence River, conditions vary widely within New York. More than 200 types of ecological communities have been identified in the state.

Wildlife biologists divide the state into ecozones, which are regions with similar climate, elevation, geology and other physical characteristics. Within an ecozone, dozens of ecosystems and ecological communities may be found.

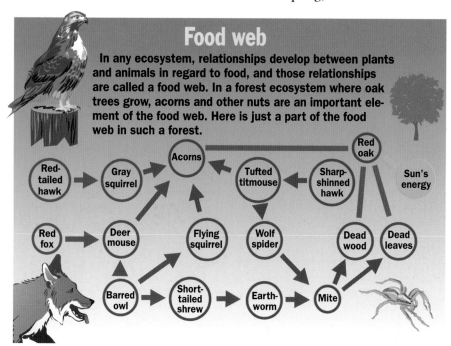

Food web

In any ecosystem, relationships develop between plants and animals in regard to food, and those relationships are called a food web. In a forest ecosystem where oak trees grow, acorns and other nuts are an important element of the food web. Here is just a part of the food web in such a forest.

Alpine meadow

About 85 acres of these meadows occur above the timberline in the higher mountain summits of the Adirondacks. The timberline is the elevation above which trees do not grow – about 4,900 feet above sea level in New York. Plants found here include Bigelow's sedge, alpine sweetgrass, Labrador tea and bearberry willows. Birds seen here include dark-eyed juncos and white-throated sparrows. Examples of alpine meadows can be found on Algonquin Peak in Essex County.

Successional old field

When farm land or cleared fields are allowed to grow free, grasses and wildflowers are typically the first plants to take root, followed by shrubs and trees. Wildflowers found here include New England asters, dandelions and Queen Anne's lace. Animals seen here include eastern cottontails, meadow voles, field sparrows, red foxes, woodchucks and white-tailed deer. Successional old fields occur statewide.

Spruce-northern hardwood forest

These forests occur on lower mountain slopes and upper parts of relatively flat regions. Trees found here include red spruces, red and sugar maples, beeches and yellow birches. Smaller plants include hobblebush, wood-sorrel, wood ferns and shining clubmoss. Birds found here include yellow-bellied flycatchers, white-throated sparrows and pileated woodpeckers. An example of a spruce-northern hardwood forest can be found in the Five Ponds Wilderness Area in Herkimer County.

Floodplain forest

These are forests in areas along rivers that regularly flood. The trees found in them typically include silver and red maples, cottonwoods, butternuts, sycamores, black willows and swamp white oaks. Plants seen here include jewelweed, Virginia creeper and poison ivy. Birds include red-bellied woodpeckers and tufted titmice. Examples of floodplain forests can be found on Doyles Islands in Delaware County and in the South Bay Creek wetlands in Washington County.

Tidal river

This is a river that flows into the ocean so that there is some mixing of fresh and salt water and some rise and fall of the water level due to ocean tides. Fish found here include Atlantic tomcods, rainbow smelt, striped bass, American shad and spottail shiners. An example of a tidal river is the Hudson River from New York City to Troy.

Confined river

This is the portion of a stream where pools, riffles and flat-water runs occur and where there might be waterfalls and springs. The water is usually fast-flowing and clear. Fish found here include creek chub, common shiners, darters and minnows. Rainbow trout, brown trout and smallmouth bass may have been introduced. Plants found here include waterweed and pondweed. Examples of confined rivers are the French Creek in Chautauqua County and the East Branch Fish Creek in Lewis County.

Appalachian Oak-hickory forest

This is a forest of hardwood trees that is usually found on ridgetops and upper slopes. Trees found here include red, white or black oaks, with some hickories. Oaks produce acorns, so animals seen here include those that feed on acorns, such as gray and flying squirrels, deer mice and wild turkeys. Examples of this type of forest can be found in the Finger Lakes National Forest in Schuyler County and in Long Eddy in Delaware County.

Maritime dunes

These coastal sand dunes are dominated by grasses and low shrubs, including beachgrass. Dusty miller, sedge, seaside goldenrod, beach heath and rugosa roses might also be found. If there are trees, they might be pitch pines or post oaks. Birds seen here include short-eared owls. Examples of maritime dunes can be found at the Fire Island National Seashore in Suffolk County.

Urban vacant lot

Vacant lots in villages and cities can become home to a range of wildlife. Trees found here include trees-of-heaven and Norway maples. Wildflowers found here include Queen Anne's lace, dock and goldenrod. Birds found here include starlings, house sparrows and pigeons. Norway rats may also be seen. Vacant lots occur statewide.

Pumpkinseed – 4 to 8 in.,
typical length for adults –
fresh water

White perch – 8 to 10 in. –
fresh and salt water

Smallmouth bass –
8 to 15 in. – fresh water

Rainbow trout – 10 to 25 in. –
fresh and salt water

Striped bass – 18 to 45 in. –
fresh and salt water

The earth was made for fish. Nearly 71 percent of the earth's surface is covered by the oceans, and about 3.5 percent of the land surface is covered with fresh water. Uncounted billions of fish call all this water home.

New York, with the Atlantic Ocean to the southeast, the Great Lakes to the northwest and thousands of lakes, rivers and streams in between, can claim a great variety of fish life. In fact, more than 165 species of fish can be found in the fresh waters of the state's lakes, ponds and streams. And hundreds of other species of ocean-going fish can be found along the state's coastline.

One can find Pacific salmon and northern pike in Lake Ontario, pumpkinseeds and bullheads in almost any large pond, striped bass and American shad in the Hudson River and bluefish and winter flounder in Long Island Sound.

Some fish, such as the yellow perch and the pumpkinseed, are found only in freshwater habitats. You will find the halibut and great white shark only in the salt water of the ocean. However, the striped killifish and the mummichog spend most of their time in a mix of fresh and salt water, such as where a river empties into the ocean.

Some fish split their time between fresh water and salt water. Sea lampreys are hatched from eggs laid in freshwater rivers and streams, but they spend most of their lives in the Atlantic Ocean before returning upriver to spawn, or produce eggs. The American eel does just the opposite, laying its eggs in salt water but living mostly in fresh water.

Fish evolved well before land animals, first appearing nearly 500 million years ago. Most scientists believe land animals can claim fish as their ancestors. They believe amphibians, such as salamanders and frogs, evolved directly from fish; reptiles, such as snakes and turtles, evolved from amphibians; and birds and mammals, including human beings, evolved separately from reptiles.

Fish breathe underwater by drawing oxygen from water as it passes over their gills. Sharks are fish, but whales (including dolphins and porpoises, which are kinds of whales) are mammals. Whales breathe air into their lungs like human beings, holding their breath when they submerge. Some whales can stay submerged for more than an hour on one breath.

Most fish are among those animals whose reproductive strategy is to lay lots of eggs and then abandon them. Enough usually survive so that their species will survive. Fish usually produce thousands or even millions of eggs each season. A female bluefin tuna may produce 10 million eggs in a single year.

Some sharks lay eggs, but others give birth to live young that hatch from eggs inside the mother and then eat other eggs or developing young before being born.

Trophy fish

Here are the record weights, in pounds, as of May 2002 for some species of fish caught in New York inland and coastal waters.

Pumpkinseed – 1.56
Yellow perch – 3.5
Smallmouth bass – 8.25
Bluefish – 25
Rainbow trout – 26.94
Channel catfish – 30
Lake trout – 39.5
Carp – 50.25
Striped bass – 76
Cod – 85
Swordfish – 492.25
Bluefin tuna – 1,071
Tiger shark – 1,087
White shark – 3,450

Nothing seems so alive as a pond in summer. A small pond just a few dozen feet across can seem to support more species of wildlife than a whole forest – frogs, birds, turtles, fish, insects and wildflowers all crowding in together, like people at a community swimming pool in August.

Mallards

In fact, ponds are communities, and like most communities they have distinct neighborhoods. There are some species that prefer the shore edges, while others like deeper water. Some stay on the water's surface, and others rarely leave the pond's bottom.

For a plant, one neighborhood may provide a better combination of sunlight and nutrients than another. For an animal, a certain neighborhood may increase its chances of survival because it offers more food and protection from predators than another neighborhood.

Freshwater ponds tend to be home to many of the same plant and animal species no matter where you go in the region, from blue flag irises on the shore to pickerelweed in the shallow water and fragrant water lilies floating in deeper water. You might see mallards paddling across the water or a kingfisher perched in the trees, ready to dive into the water to catch a passing fish.

Life in a pond follows a seasonal clock. In January, a pond is mostly asleep. Only a few animals stir under the thick ice that covers it – perhaps a muskrat feeding on the remains of water plants or a yellow perch slowly gliding along.

By March, with the sun higher in the sky, the ice around the pond edges may be turning to slush. Red-winged blackbird males return to establish nesting territories around the pond. The eggs of insects hatch in the mud along the

Blue flag

shore, and water lilies are growing new shoots. Finally, the ice melts completely.

In April, fish feed on developing insects in the shallows. Turtles bask on logs and rocks to warm up. In May, leaves appear on trees around the pond, and mallards are building their nests on dry land close to the pond and laying eggs.

By June, the pond has come fully to life. Mayflies are hatching in great numbers. The young of red-winged blackbirds are being hatched, and the chorusing of bullfrogs and green frogs can be heard at night.

In July, microscopic life in the water becomes thick. Dragonflies hover over the water, mallards and their young feed on submerged plants, and muskrats feed on plants in the shallows. There is motion everywhere in and around the pond.

In August, things grow quieter. The task of reproduction for most pond wildlife is completed, so their main job of the summer is over. The water may turn green from algae growth. The heads of frogs sit motionless above the water, like tiny islands.

In September and October, many birds abandon the pond to fly south for the winter. At the first frost, leaves on many pond plants turn brown and start to die. Water lilies may break off from their roots and float to shore, pushed by chilly autumn gusts.

As the days grow shorter and the nights grow colder, frogs and turtles move to the bottom of the pond to hibernate. Muskrats grow less active.

Eventually, ice begins to form along the pond edges. It will gradually grow thicker, working its way to the center until the pond is completely frozen over, waiting for spring and that time in its cycle when it will come to life once again.

Pond neighborhoods

Here are some of the wildlife species that can be found in different neighborhoods of a pond in summer.

Air
Kingfisher, dragonfly, damselfly, mosquito, little brown bat, mayfly

Shore
Bullfrog, green frog, blue flag, raccoon, purple loosestrife, weeping willow, green ash, painted turtle

Shallow water
Green heron, great blue heron, bluegill, pickerelweed, cattail, water snake, duckweed, grassy arrowhead, muskrat

Water surface
Whirligig beetle, mallard, water strider, springtail, water lily, bullfrog, green frog

Deeper water
Yellow perch, beaver

Pond bottom
Snapping turtle, bullhead, leech, crayfish, dragonfly nymph

The oceans were home to living things well before the land was. And just as land animals have evolved to take forms that increase their species' chance of survival, so have marine creatures.

Finding food and trying not to be something else's food are two of the main reasons why different forms of life have the different forms they do. To be fast on land so that you can escape predators or so that you can be a predator yourself, you need strong legs and a sleek runner's body, like an antelope or a cheetah. If you're not going to be a fast runner, you need something else that protects you, like the tough outer shell of a turtle. You can also be well protected if you have the huge size of an elephant or the small size of a spider, which can hide from predators in tiny openings.

In the water, the same rules hold true. A marine creature survives best if it has speed or a protective physical feature.

To be fast swimmers, many marine animals, such as sharks and dolphins, have smooth, torpedo-shaped bodies so that they can cut easily through the water. Many of the slow movers, such as clams, lobsters and horseshoe crabs,

Harbor seal

Horseshoe crab

have a hard outer shell. Summer flounders have camouflage. They are flat fish that lie on the ocean bottom, settling into the sand and changing their color to match their surroundings.

The huge size of whales makes them safe from most marine predators. And the fourspine stickleback – a very small fish, only about 2 inches in length – stays close to underwater vegetation near shorelines, where it can hide from larger predatory fish that come near.

Starfish have a unique way to increase their chances of survival. A predator may take a bite out of a starfish, but even if it loses four of its five arms and most of its central disk, a starfish can still regrow its entire body.

Laws also protect some ocean animals. Several decades ago, seals were rare sights in New York waters. Some would occasionally take fish from fishermen's nets, so bounties were offered for dead seals. However, laws were passed protecting marine mammals, and now thousands of seals, including harbor, gray, harp, hooded and ringed seals, are seen in winter on the beaches of Long Island and on its offshore islands.

Ghost crab

Seashell collection
The shells found on beaches were once the portable homes of living marine creatures.

Northern quahog
2.5 to 4 in. – Also called hard-shelled clams, quahogs usually live in protected bays and inlets.

Eastern oyster
2 to 8 in. – Oysters are usually found below the low-tide line. They are often found in clusters.

Blue mussel
1 to 4 in. – Mussels often form great colonies, attaching to rocks, shells, wood pilings or other solid structures near or below the low-tide mark.

Common periwinkle
1 in. or less – Periwinkles often attach to rocks or vegetation in the zone between low and high tide where they feed on algae.

Soft-shelled clam
1 to 5.5 in. – These shellfish, also known as steamer clams, are usually found in sand or mud.

Channeled whelk
3 to 8 in. – Whelks are sea snails, and channeled whelks are found from Cape Cod to Florida on sandy or muddy ocean bottoms.

Atlantic bay scallop
1.5 to 4 in. – These scallops normally live in the shallow water of protected bays where sea grasses grow.

Knobbed whelk
4 to 9 in. – These marine snails feed on clams. They are typically found in sand in shallow water.

Humpback whale

Humpback whale breaching

Whale hunters once sailed the ocean off Long Island. Now those same waters are the destination for the ships of whale watchers.

Finbacks and humpbacks, minke whales and right whales – some 25 species of whales have been seen off New York's seacoast in the last few decades.

Whales are divided into two groups – baleen whales and toothed whales. Finback and humpback whales are baleen whales, which means they capture small fish by straining them out of water using features (baleens) that hang from their upper jaws and look like the teeth of a comb. The water can pass through, but fish do not.

Killer whales, sperm whales, dolphins and porpoises are toothed whales. They capture prey with their teeth and strong jaws. While fish are their primary food, killer whales may also hunt seals, dolphins, squid or even other whales.

The most common baleen whales to be seen in New York's ocean waters are finback and humpback whales. Only rarely seen, perhaps once every four or five years, is a blue whale. The largest animal that has ever lived on earth, the blue whale can be more than 100 feet long and can weigh 300,000 pounds – more than 100 cars.

Humpback whales are regularly seen in summer in shallow waters around New York's coast, including Long Island Sound and Gardiner's Bay. They are slow swimmers, but they can be quite acrobatic, jumping out of the water at times, an action called breaching. For whale watchers, to see a whale that is breaching is a treasured sight.

It's estimated there are about 2,000 to 4,000 humpback whales remaining in the western North Atlantic.

Whales are mammals and, like land-dwelling mammals, they give birth to live young, they have lungs and they breathe air.

Although some whales can remain underwater for more than an hour on one breath, they all must come to the surface periodically to breathe. When a whale does surface, it forcefully exhales by shooting out a spout of air and water vapor from a "blowhole" on the top of its head. The spout from a blue whale may rise more than 30 feet.

It is a general rule in nature that the larger an animal is then the longer it tends to live. (Turtles, some of which can live a century, are one exception.) Whales can live long lives. Humpback whales may live 50 years, and some finbacks and right whales may live 90 years or more.

Dolphin or porpoise?

Dolphins, with their long snouts, are often more playful than porpoises and will usually venture closer to people and boats. Porpoises have shorter noses and tend to be shyer creatures than dolphins.

Whales of New York coastal waters

Minke whale
20 to 30 ft. – These whales sometimes feed near coasts and may swim into bays and estuaries.

Atlantic white-sided dolphin
7 to 9 ft. – These dolphins, which are a type of whale, sometimes travel in large schools numbering as many as 1,000 individuals.

Humpback whale
40 to 50 ft. – Humpbacks, which can weigh 50 tons, are probably the favorite of whale watchers. When they breach and fall back into the water, the sound can be heard for miles.

Finback or fin whale
50 to 70 ft. – Second in size to blue whales, finbacks are streamlined and can swim up to 30 miles per hour. Despite their size, they are capable of leaping out of the water.

Right whale
35 to 50 ft. – There may be only 300 of these whales left in the world due to overhunting. Whalers called them the "right" whale to hunt because they were slow swimmers and floated when dead.

Impressionist painters would not have gotten far without wildflowers.

Wildflowers were art before there was art – dashes of color on canvases of windblown meadows, craggy mountainsides and darkened forest floors.

Many seem to have been named by poets – Jack-in-the-pulpit, Queen Anne's lace, butter and eggs, yellow lady's slipper.

But as unplanned as a scattering of wildflowers may seem, where and when they bloom and the colors and shapes they take follow a general logic. Much of that logic has to do with helping each species of wildflower find its own place in the world.

If all wildflowers bloomed at the same time, grew in the same soil and sunlight conditions and attracted the same pollinators, the fierce competition would mean that only a few species would survive. So wildflowers evolved to be specialists. Some grow only in wet areas, some grow only in dry areas. Some thrive in valleys and others on mountainsides. Some can grow where there is a lot of sunlight, as in a meadow, while others can grow where there is little of it, as on a forest floor.

To further reduce competition, wildflowers also evolved to bloom at different times of year. Common violets bloom from April to June, but most asters don't bloom until September or October.

The beauty of wildflowers is not something created to please the human eye. It actually evolved to appeal to pollinators – butterflies, bees, ants, moths and even small

Wild columbine

Wild lupine

birds, such as hummingbirds. The splashy and bold colors of some wildflowers are like neon signs outside a row of stores that aim to catch the eyes of passing customers. The fragrances the flowers give off and the sweet nectar produced inside the flowers are also intended as attractions to pollinators.

A wildflower must get the pollen that the male part of the flower creates to the female part of another wildflower of the same species so that seeds can be created. Pollinators are the pollen carriers.

If a butterfly visits a flower to feed on the nectar deep inside the flower, tiny grains of pollen may stick to it and be carried to the next flower it visits.

The varied shapes and colors of wildflowers also evolved to let a pollinator know exactly what kind of flower it is visiting. Most pollinators can recognize certain shapes and patterns of color, so if they like the nectar they find at a flower, they will know to visit that same type of flower again. In this way, pollen from a buttercup has a way of getting to another buttercup, rather than ending up on a wild geranium.

The bull's-eye shape of many flowers evolved to guide the pollinator to the nectar. "Here it is – right at the center," this shape seems to say. Other wildflowers have a shape like the end of a trumpet for the same reason. "The nectar is right inside here – you can't miss it," this shape seems to say.

In New York, there are nearly 1,500 species of wildflowers that can be seen through the seasons.

Wildflower or weed?

There is no official definition for which is which. When people do not like a wildflower for some reason, they may think of it as a weed. Some people think dandelions are weeds because they can take over a lawn. But others like their colorful flowers and think of them as wildflowers. In New York, oxeye daisies are a favorite wildflower of many, but they are thought of as unwanted weeds by dairy farmers because cows may refuse to graze on them.

Turk's-cap lily

Yellow lady's slipper

Fragrant water lily

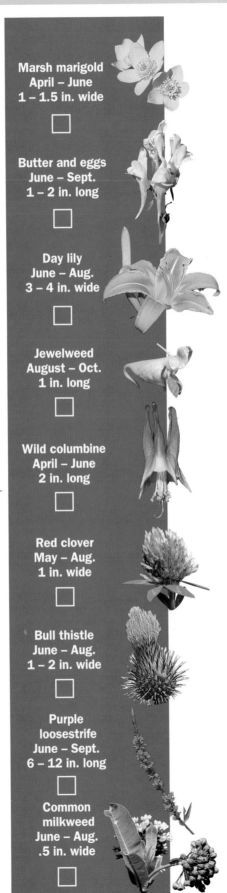
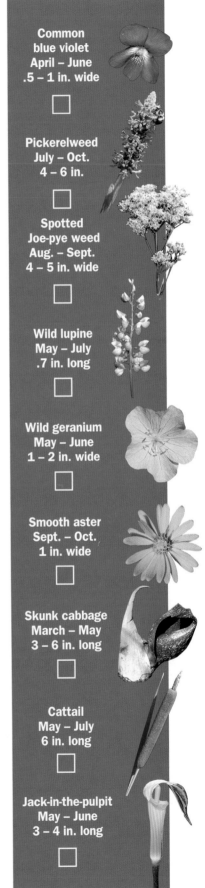

CHECKLIST
Common wildflowers of New York

Oxeye daisy
June – Aug.
1 – 3 in. wide
☐

Daisy fleabane
June – July
1 in. wide
☐

Queen Anne's lace
June – Sept.
2 – 6 in. wide
(cluster width)
☐

Fragrant water lily
June – Sept.
3 – 6 in. wide
☐

Tall goldenrod
Aug. – Oct.
.2 in. long
☐

Common dandelion
March – Sept.
1.5 in. wide
☐

Black-eyed Susan
June – Sept.
2 – 3 in. wide
☐

Common buttercup
May – June
1 in. wide
☐

Marsh marigold
April – June
1 – 1.5 in. wide
☐

Butter and eggs
June – Sept.
1 – 2 in. long
☐

Day lily
June – Aug.
3 – 4 in. wide
☐

Jewelweed
August – Oct.
1 in. long
☐

Wild columbine
April – June
2 in. long
☐

Red clover
May – Aug.
1 in. wide
☐

Bull thistle
June – Aug.
1 – 2 in. wide
☐

Purple loosestrife
June – Sept.
6 – 12 in. long
☐

Common milkweed
June – Aug.
.5 in. wide
☐

Common blue violet
April – June
.5 – 1 in. wide
☐

Pickerelweed
July – Oct.
4 – 6 in.
☐

Spotted Joe-pye weed
Aug. – Sept.
4 – 5 in. wide
☐

Wild lupine
May – July
.7 in. long
☐

Wild geranium
May – June
1 – 2 in. wide
☐

Smooth aster
Sept. – Oct.
1 in. wide
☐

Skunk cabbage
March – May
3 – 6 in. long
☐

Cattail
May – July
6 in. long
☐

Jack-in-the-pulpit
May – June
3 – 4 in. long
☐

To much of the world, the words "New York" bring to mind only the sophisticated city. But the true representative of the state is probably the primitive forest.

About 62 percent of the state is covered with forests. It's estimated that 10 billion trees at least an inch in diameter at breast height can be found in New York, from red maples, black locusts and white pines to red oaks, black cherries and white birches.

However, a little more than a century ago, farm fields, not forests, were the dominant feature of New York's landscape. In the 1800s, small farms were found throughout the state. Less than a quarter of the state was covered with forests in the late 1800s.

With the completion of the Erie Canal in 1825 and the building of railroads in the mid-1800s, an easy passage to the Midwest was created. Many New York farmers who had fields with poor soil abandoned their land for the more easily farmed prairies out west. The Great Depression of the 1930s convinced many more farmers to leave their land.

Faced with so many abandoned fields, the state began programs to plant tree seedlings in fields in the 1920s. In addition, there was an effort to buy land for state forests. Today, there are more than 700,000 acres of state forests in New York.

However, many fields grew into forests on their own. When a field is abandoned, or when a hurricane or a fire creates an area of open land, there is a predictable order in which seedlings will take root in the clearing. It may take more than two centuries for a forest that develops there to grow to maturity.

In upstate New York, eastern white pine is often the first species of tree to become established in an open field. Many grazing animals, such as deer, prefer to eat the seedlings of hardwood trees, such as maples, rather than those of softwoods, such as pines. (A

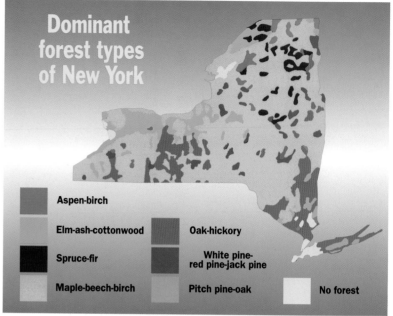

Dominant forest types of New York

- Aspen-birch
- Elm-ash-cottonwood
- Spruce-fir
- Maple-beech-birch
- Oak-hickory
- White pine-red pine-jack pine
- Pitch pine-oak
- No forest

softwood tree is just what its name suggests. The wood is softer than that of a hardwood.)

Once the pine forest begins maturing, the hardwoods will slowly take root beneath the umbrella formed by the pines. Because the hardwoods can grow in shade, they can flourish on the forest floor. But because pine cannot easily grow in shade, pine seedlings on the forest floor do not prosper. Eventually, the tall pines may die and the smaller hardwoods will replace them.

Today, the most common trees in the state are red maples, making up about 18 percent of all trees greater than 5 inches in diameter at breast height. Next are sugar maples (14 percent), followed by hemlocks (8 percent).

As landscape and climate conditions change in New York, so will the types of trees you see. In the sandy soils of Long Island, pitch pines and white oaks are among the most abundant trees. On the cool slopes of the Adirondack Mountains, spruces, maples, firs, beeches and birches tend to be the dominant trees.

Is fall foliage just an accident?

Perhaps nature's most brilliant artistic touch, the scarlets and golds of autumn leaves may also be one of nature's most beautiful accidents.

The startling colors of fall are certainly admired by human beings. But the colors seem to defy one of nature's primary laws, since they are of no use to the trees themselves.

Most plants and animals have the features they have because those features help them survive in the world. But what use is a colorful leaf to a tree in autumn since the leaf is just about to die and fall to the ground?

Some scientists believe that autumn colors may have begun as an accident, the unexpected result of the chemical changes a tree goes through as it prepares to lose its leaves each fall.

But even if it was an accident, since this coloring causes no harm to the trees, there is no reason for trees to lose this process. If the coloring did cause harm, those species of trees whose leaves changed color might have become extinct by now, and only the trees whose leaves didn't change color might be alive today.

CHECKLIST
Common trees of New York

Sugar maple
typical height
60 – 80 ft.
☐

Red maple
50 – 80 ft.
☐

Northern
red oak
60 – 80 ft.
☐

Yellow birch
60 – 80 ft.
☐

Paper birch
50 – 70 ft.
☐

Black cherry
50 – 70 ft.
☐

American
beech
60 – 80 ft.
☐

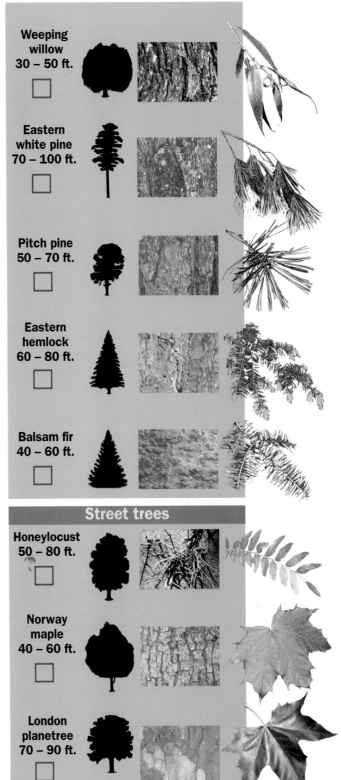

Weeping
willow
30 – 50 ft.
☐

Eastern
white pine
70 – 100 ft.
☐

Pitch pine
50 – 70 ft.
☐

Eastern
hemlock
60 – 80 ft.
☐

Balsam fir
40 – 60 ft.
☐

Street trees

Honeylocust
50 – 80 ft.
☐

Norway
maple
40 – 60 ft.
☐

London
planetree
70 – 90 ft.
☐

New York's champion trees are determined by this formula: The sum of the circumference at breast height in inches, the height in feet, and one quarter the average crown width in feet. Here are the champions for some species, their home counties, circumferences, heights and crown widths. An eastern cottonwood is currently the state's champion tree.

Cottonwood – Rensselaer, 365 in., 98 ft., 100 ft. = 488 pts.
Red maple – Madison, 255 in., 135 ft., 108 ft. = 417 pts.
Red oak – Albany, 204 in., 114 ft., 84 ft. = 339 pts.
Sugar maple – Madison, 235 in., 68 ft., 60 ft. = 318 pts.
Weeping willow – Schoharie, 204 in., 63 ft., 72 ft. = 285 pts.
Honeylocust – Schoharie, 171 in., 95 ft., 60 ft. = 281 pts.

They are the silent observers of history. New York's oldest living trees were alive when Native Americans dominated the region, when the Revolutionary War was fought, and when electric lights first appeared.

Indeed, there are tens of thousands of acres of old-growth trees in the state. Some of these ancient trees may be 500 and possibly 600 years old.

But if you think that the oldest trees in a forest are always the largest trees, you'd be wrong. Perhaps the oldest trees in New York are some of the most inconspicuous, usually growing to a height of less than 80 feet. They are black gum trees, also called black tupelo or pepperidge trees.

Only in the last decade have people who study old-growth trees recognized just how long this wetland species can survive. It had been thought that the oldest trees in the Northeast were no more than 550 years old. However, in New Hampshire in 1999, a black gum was found that was 626 years old.

How do scientists determine the age of a tree? By counting its rings. A tree grows new wood around the outside of its trunk each year. In the late spring and early summer, when there is usually more moisture in the ground, the wood is light in appearance. In late summer and early fall, when conditions are usually drier, the wood being added tends to be darker. This alternating light and dark wood creates rings that can be seen when the tree falls in a storm or is cut.

Eastern white pine

To count the rings of a living tree, a scientist drills out a pencil-thin "core," a rod of wood extracted from the trunk on which the rings can be seen.

There is no firm definition for an old-growth tree, but for many species, living 150 to 200 years can put them in that category.

In New York, much of the land was cleared for farming in Colonial times, even the lower slopes of mountains. So most of the old-growth trees that exist today are found in the higher elevations of mountains or in places that people can't easily reach, such as on islands or steep slopes.

Among the long-lived species in New York, in addition to black gum trees, are eastern white pines, eastern hemlocks, white cedars, balsam firs, red spruces, sugar maples and American beeches.

The greatest wealth of old trees in New York is in the Adirondack Mountains, as many as 200,000 acres by some estimates. Adirondack Park is such a vast area that new stands are always being discovered. The region may have more undiscovered old-growth trees than any state east of the Mississippi River.

While 500 years' longevity is impressive for New York, it wouldn't raise an eyebrow in some other regions. There is a bald cypress in North Carolina that is estimated to be 1,700 years old, the champion for old growth in the eastern United States.

The champions for the nation, and perhaps the world, are bristlecone pines that grow on the barren windy slopes of the southwestern United States. Some of those may be nearly 5,000 years old.

Old-growth trees of New York
Some major stands

Adirondack Mountains

Catskill Mountains

Adirondacks
An estimated 60,000 to more than 200,000 acres of red spruce, balsam fir and American mountain-ash

Catskills
An estimated 10,000 to 20,000 acres of red spruce, balsam fir, paper birch, yellow birch, red maple, black cherry and American beech

Livingston and Ontario counties
Around Hemlock and Canadice lakes, about 1,000 acres of eastern hemlock, scarlet oak, red oak and white pine

Cattaraugus County
In Allegany State park, 770 acres of eastern hemlock and northern hardwood trees

Ulster, Sullivan and Orange counties
On the ridge of the Shawangunk Mountains, 5,000 acres of dwarf pitch pine

Suffolk County
On Gardiner's Island, many stands of white oak

Suffolk County
In Sunken Forest on a barrier island in Fire Island National Seashore, 20 to 30 acres of American holly, black gum, sassafras and shadbush

In weather not fit for man or beast, the beasts and other forms of wildlife manage to do a pretty good job of surviving in winter.

Through the ages, plants and animals have gained a variety of tricks for getting through even the most severe winter weather.

Some animals hibernate, sleeping through the worst of it. Others know how and where to avoid biting winds and freezing temperatures and where to find food in a pinch.

Birds can seem the most vulnerable of animals in winter, but they often ride out storms perched high up inside the layered branches of dense evergreen trees, sheltered from the snow and wind, sleeping or eating insects they find in the bark and under limbs. Their feathers offer natural protection from the cold. They can also fluff up their feathers with air for even greater insulation.

Woodchucks and bats hibernate through the winter. Beavers spend the winter awake in their lodges. Rabbits take refuge in tunnels under snow-covered shrubs or in abandoned woodchuck holes. For these and other mammals, their fur is their winter coat.

For coyotes, red foxes, bobcats and a variety of birds of prey that choose not to migrate, such as red-tailed hawks, winter in this region is business as usual as they prowl and patrol the countryside for a meal. Snow can

Mallards

actually benefit them since it can make prey stand out.

For both plants and animals, the greatest danger of severe cold is that it can freeze water. When water does freeze, it expands and forms sharp-edged ice crystals. The cells of all living things are filled with water, and if that water turns to ice, it can puncture the cell walls, causing damage or even death.

Perhaps the most fantastic trick for surviving freezing temperatures is the one used by some frogs. Many frogs spend the winter on land, buried beneath leaves on the forest floor. But it may become so cold that even these places have freezing temperatures. To cope with such conditions, treefrogs, wood frogs and even spring peepers have found a way to turn to ice in winter, their bodies nearly frozen solid, and still survive. With just a few warm spring days, they will thaw out and begin to do the things frogs normally do in the spring.

How do they do it? They create chemical "seeds" within their body cavities but outside the cells of their organs and other body tissues. When the temperature drops below freezing, ice crystals will form around the seeds so that the water inside the cells does not freeze. Up to two-thirds of a frog's body water can freeze, yet it can remain alive because its cells are unharmed.

Winter survival strategies

Sugar maple

Leaf-bearing trees, such as maples, shed their frost-sensitive leaves in the fall and move a lot of their water and nutrients – their sap – into their roots, away from freezing temperatures.

White pine

The needles of evergreens, such as pines, are not very sensitive to cold because of natural antifreeze molecules within their cells. Also, the cells contain low amounts of water.

Honey bee

Honey bees form large clusters inside their hives and create heat by shivering or beating their wings. To prevent the bees on the outside of the cluster from freezing to death, those on the inside change places with them from time to time.

Day lily

Some plants, like corn, die completely at the first frost, leaving their seeds behind to produce new plants in the spring. In others, like day lilies, the parts above ground die when winter arrives, but underground roots and stems live to grow again in the spring.

Snapping turtle

These cold-blooded creatures will often sit in the unfrozen mud at the bottom of a pond. There, they lower their heart beat and other body processes until they have almost no signs of life.

Flounder

Flounders can produce their own antifreeze to keep their body fluids from freezing. Since salt water freezes at a lower temperature than fresh water, they may overwinter in water with subfreezing temperatures.

It's not called the urban jungle for nothing. A city can be teeming with animals, from birds to bats to butterflies, and people who live there may be unaware of most.

That's because many animals that do choose to live where there are great concentrations of people eventually learn ways to live their lives without attracting notice.

There are some animals, though, that have the personality – and the agility – to live among people but to stay out of their way. Gray squirrels and pigeons can seem to be acrobats of city sidewalks as they avoid being trampled.

Still other animals thrive in cities because they are terrific survivors. Norway rats and German cockroaches, two species people especially dislike, have managed to survive despite the most intense efforts imaginable to eliminate them.

But even in urban areas, there can be rural landscapes in the form of city parks. They are often havens for animals. For birds especially, a park's greenery can be an oasis in the middle of a desert of concrete and steel. In fact, concentrations of some birds can be higher in a good-sized park than they are in the outlying rural areas.

That's especially true in spring and fall when birds migrate. They have to stop and rest periodically, and if they are flying over a densely populated area with lots of buildings and little greenery, a park will stand out for them like the bull's-eye of a target. That's why Central Park in New York City, with 843 acres, is such a prime bird-watching destination for people. Nearly 300 species of birds have been seen in Central Park, with many of them spotted only during the migration periods.

While Manhattan is an island, Syracuse, Buffalo, Albany

House sparrow nest

and other large cities in the state are not. They are more likely to be entered by wild animals, such as raccoons, opossums and skunks, especially at night. Larger animals may also become established in urban parks and range out from there.

White-tailed deer have taken up residence in the 264-acre Tifft Nature Preserve in Buffalo and frequently venture into surrounding neighborhoods. Similarly, wild turkeys are established in the 80-acre Tivoli Preserve in Albany and will wander into nearby areas.

The breeding season will also send animals into areas where they are not usually found – primarily males, which may wander widely in search of females. Black bears have been frequently seen within the city limits of Binghamton, moose have been spotted in Albany, and almost all communities in upstate New York have had deer bucks galloping through residential neighborhoods during the mating season.

For some animals, the feeding opportunities in cities can be greater than in the deep forest. Peregrine falcons were originally a mountain species. They would build their nests on cliff ledges and use that vantage point to spot prey, usually other birds, which they would attack in flight.

In the modern world, peregrine falcons find the man-made cliffs of cities serve them just as well. They will nest on the roofs and window ledges of tall buildings or on the girders of bridges and then hunt the canyons of the city for pigeons and other birds. In New York City, nearly a dozen falcon nests have been established. Buffalo, Rochester and greater Albany have also been home to nesting falcons.

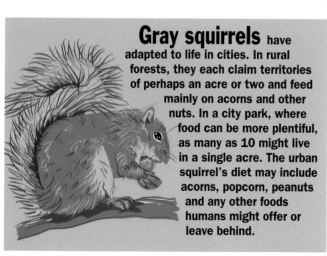

Gray squirrels have adapted to life in cities. In rural forests, they each claim territories of perhaps an acre or two and feed mainly on acorns and other nuts. In a city park, where food can be more plentiful, as many as 10 might live in a single acre. The urban squirrel's diet may include acorns, popcorn, peanuts and any other foods humans might offer or leave behind.

Peregrine falcon

Central Park, New York City, looking north

Imagine mountains as high as Mount Everest. Imagine erupting volcanoes. Imagine mile-high glaciers or frozen snowswept plains.

You are imagining landscapes that could have been seen in New York at different times in its history.

Hard to believe? Not for geologists. They know that the appearance of every region on earth has changed over time. They also know that now is a quiet time in the geologic cycle of the Northeast, a momentary calm amid the violent upheavals that have marked the history of the region's landscape.

The earth's crust, or surface layer, is made up of vast rock plates that form the continents and the ocean floor. There are about a dozen large plates and many smaller ones covering the earth's surface, arranged like pieces in a jigsaw puzzle.

The crust under the oceans may have an average thickness of just 4 or 5 miles. The crust of the continental plates is about 20 miles thick on average.

Essentially, the plates "float" on a layer of denser rock, called the mantle, deeper within the earth. The earth's core has a temperature of perhaps 8,000° Fahrenheit, and this great heat creates circulating currents of molten rock within the mantle, which slowly push the crustal

Roadcut, Catskill, N.Y.

plates along.

The plates typically move a few inches a year, sometimes coming together and sometimes moving apart. This is called continental drift.

Even at such a slow speed, though, when these massive plates push against each other, geologic fireworks happen. Mountains gradually rise into the air, volcanoes may erupt and earthquakes might rumble.

That's what's happening currently in the western United States. The Pacific and North American plates are slowly sliding by each other, grinding together along their edges. About 65 million years ago, when the plates were pushing right into each other, this process created the Rocky Mountains, which are considered "young" mountains. (Scientists believe the earth is about 4.6 billion years old.)

New York is also part of the North American plate, but for nearly 190 million years this plate has been separating from the plate that is next to it on the east, the one on which Africa is located. So there are no strong geologic pressures on New York's part of the plate to create or enlarge mountains. As a result, the magnificent mountains that were formed in the state during a collision of continental plates 460 million years ago have spent these millions of years being slowly eroded by the weather.

Boundaries of major plates of the earth's crust

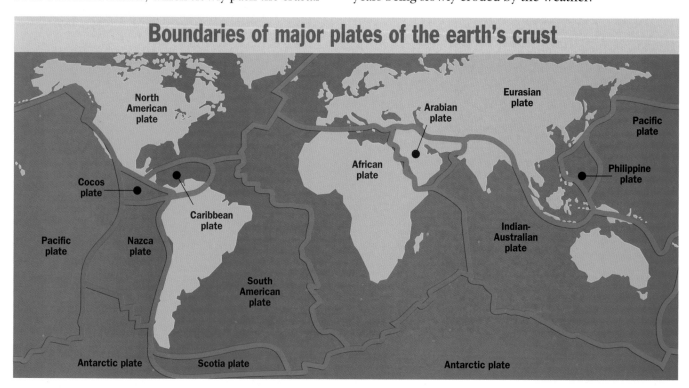

Drifting continents

Three times in the last 500 million years, the East Coast of North America has collided with other continental plates. These collisions did much to shape the landscape of New York.

Although continental plates may move only inches a year, their masses are so great that once they come together they may continue to push against each other for millions of years, creating mountains, earthquakes and volcanoes in the region of the collision.

The theory of continental drift became widely accepted by scientists only in the 1960s. So the position of the continents through geologic history is still being estimated.

500 million years ago

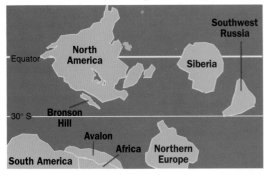

New York is on a continent lying on the equator. Trees, plants and animals have not yet appeared on land. Primitive life is still developing in the oceans. The first fishlike creatures appear in water. Less than a foot in length, they lack jaws but they do have backbones, perhaps the first animals that are vertebrates.

The oxygen content of the earth's atmosphere is rising sharply, but it will be another 100 million years before air-breathing land animals evolve.

Drifting north toward early North America is a plate covered with volcanoes, called Bronson Hill by geologists, that is about to collide with what will become the East Coast.

460 million years ago

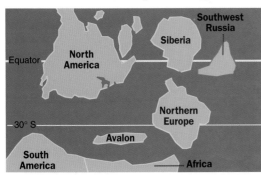

Bronson Hill collides with the North American coast, pushing up layers of rock that form the Taconic Mountains in eastern New York and western New England. These peaks are as high as the Himalayas are today, but gradually wind and rain erode them.

Rain falling on the western slopes of the mountains creates rushing rivers that fill with eroded debris. The rivers flow out into New York, laying down a thick wide blanket of mud, sand and gravel.

Meanwhile, Avalon, another plate, has broken free of the united African-South American continent and is drifting north.

380 million years ago

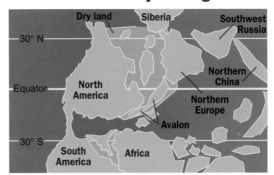

Avalon collides with North America, folding up layers of land like an accordion in New England. There is little rising of land in New York, but when the New England peaks erode, rivers carrying debris deposit this eroded material over New York, creating the sediments that will become the bedrock of the Catskill region. Much of the state is now covered by a shallow inland sea. Primitive fish fill this and other seas, and plants are starting to flourish on land.

300 million years ago

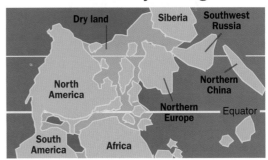

190 million years ago

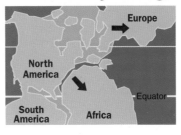

Africa collides with North America about 300 million years ago. All seven continents become joined in a single vast continent, called Pangaea by geologists. The collision probably has little effect on the landscape of New York.

About 190 million years ago, Africa starts to pull away from North America.

The first dinosaurs appear about 230 million years ago, but they are relatively small, just a few feet in height. The first mammals, not much larger than mice, appear about the same time. However, the first birds and flowers will not appear for another 80 million years.

The rock cycle

Rocks have their own life cycle. It begins on the surface of the earth when wind, rain and other natural forces break down existing rocks and other materials. The resulting particles become compressed and cemented together over the course of time to form new rocks.

When sand is turned to rock in this way, sandstone is the result. When clay, such as what is deposited on the bottom of a lake, is turned to rock, shale is the result. These two rocks are called sedimentary rocks, one of three categories of rocks along with metamorphic and igneous.

Eventually, sedimentary rocks, such as sandstone and shale, are buried by layers of other sedimentary rocks. With the heat and pressure deeper inside the earth, they can become harder, turning into metamorphic rocks, such as quartzite and slate.

Metamorphic rocks may eventually move to the surface due to earthquakes or the erosion of the land above them. But if metamorphic rocks move deeper into the earth, the higher temperatures there can turn them to molten rock. If this molten material hardens underground, it can become igneous rock, such as granite. If it surges up to the earth's surface through a volcano as lava and hardens, it will become another form of igneous rock, such as basalt.

Harsh weather and the freezing and thawing through the seasons eventually disintegrate surface rocks. These rock particles may then become part of new sedimentary rocks, continuing the cycle.

The rock collection

Sandstone
Sedimentary; formed from sand

Quartzite
Metamorphic; formed from sandstone

Shale
Sedimentary; formed from mud and clay

Slate
Metamorphic; formed from shale at low temperatures

Limestone
Sedimentary; formed from minerals such as calcite

Marble
Metamorphic; formed from limestone

Conglomerate
Sedimentary; formed from a mix of sand and pebbles

Schist
Metamorphic; often formed from shale at medium temperatures

Mineral or rock?

Minerals have crystalline structures, and they are usually made up of only a few chemical elements. For instance, diamond is made of carbon, and quartz is made of silicon and oxygen. Rocks, such as schist or granite, may be made up of combinations of minerals and bits of other rocks. While the minerals in it may have crystalline structures, the overall rock usually does not.

Gneiss
Metamorphic; formed from igneous and sedimentary rocks

Granite
Igneous; formed when molten rock cools underground

Quartz, a mineral

New York's bedrock geology

If you dig down through the loose dirt and rocks on the earth's surface, you will eventually strike solid rock, called bedrock. In coastal areas or on steep mountain slopes, you may not have to dig deeply at all to find bedrock. In river valleys, where flooding has deposited layer upon layer of silt and clay over the centuries, you might have to dig down 100 feet or more.

New York has distinct regions of bedrock, reflecting the different circumstances in which the rock was formed.

Much of the story of New York's bedrock involves the uplift of huge mountains in eastern New York and western New England as the result of continental collisions, followed by the erosion of those mountains over millions of years.

Rain hitting the western slopes of those mountains sent rivers filled with clay, silt, sand and pebbles out into central and western New York, depositing that material in wide deltas. That eroded debris eventually turned into sedimentary rock.

The remnants of the mountains in the East, including the Taconic Mountains, are primarily made up of tough metamorphic rock.

At various times during these periods of continental collisions, central and western New York were covered by shallow inland seas. As the fish and other creatures that filled the seas died, their remains and shells would fall to the sea bottom, creating layers of material that eventually turned to limestone.

The Adirondack Mountains and Long Island are part of more recent stories.

Some 20 million years ago, the region that is today the Adirondacks was probably a fairly flat plain of sedimentary bedrock. But heat deeper in the earth began to push that region up in the shape of an overturned bowl. The sedimentary rock on the surface gradually eroded away exposing the older, tougher metamorphic rock that lay beneath. As that rock continued to be pushed up, it did not easily erode, and today that rock forms the high peaks of the Adirondacks, which are still rising a fraction of an inch each year.

Long Island is the result of ice on the surface of the earth rather than heat inside it. The last ice age began about 70,000 years ago. A continental glacier that formed in Canada eventually spread all the way to Long Island. At its front edge, which ran the length of Long Island, it dropped so much gravel and sand that Long Island sits above the surface of the Atlantic Ocean today.

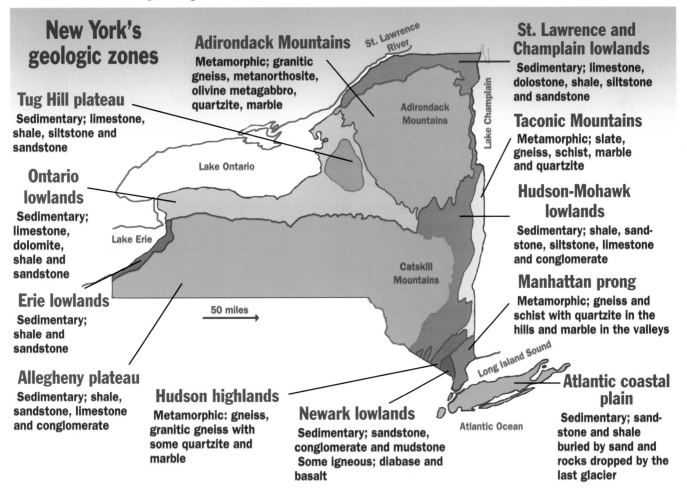

New York's geologic zones

Adirondack Mountains
Metamorphic; granitic gneiss, metanorthosite, olivine metagabbro, quartzite, marble

St. Lawrence and Champlain lowlands
Sedimentary; limestone, dolostone, shale, siltstone and sandstone

Tug Hill plateau
Sedimentary; limestone, shale, siltstone and sandstone

Taconic Mountains
Metamorphic; slate, gneiss, schist, marble and quartzite

Ontario lowlands
Sedimentary; limestone, dolomite, shale and sandstone

Hudson-Mohawk lowlands
Sedimentary; shale, sandstone, siltstone, limestone and conglomerate

Erie lowlands
Sedimentary; shale and sandstone

Manhattan prong
Metamorphic; gneiss and schist with quartzite in the hills and marble in the valleys

Allegheny plateau
Sedimentary; shale, sandstone, limestone and conglomerate

Hudson highlands
Metamorphic: gneiss, granitic gneiss with some quartzite and marble

Newark lowlands
Sedimentary; sandstone, conglomerate and mudstone Some igneous; diabase and basalt

Atlantic coastal plain
Sedimentary; sandstone and shale buried by sand and rocks dropped by the last glacier

St. Lawrence River

Adirondack Mountains

Lake Champlain

Lake Ontario

Lake Erie

Catskill Mountains

50 miles

Long Island Sound

Atlantic Ocean

Fearfully great lizards: translated from Greek, that's what "dinosauria" actually means. For nearly 165 million years, from about 230 million years ago to 65 million years ago, these legendary beasts roamed the earth.

Wherever you walk in North America, the fierce tyrannosaurus rex and the massive triceratops once walked. But while scientists find the bones of these ancient creatures in other regions, they do not find them in New York.

Bones are preserved as fossils when they are buried by sand or mud, which then turns to sedimentary rock. However, conditions in New York were not ideal for preserving the sedimentary bedrock bearing these fossils. It weathered away long ago. Geologists do find fossilized footprints of dinosaurs in New York, though.

A rock bearing the footprint of a dinosaur is like a photograph that is millions of years old. It's a snapshot in stone of events of perhaps one warm summer morning by the shores of an ancient river or lake. A dinosaur might have wandered down to the edge of the water to drink, pressing its feet into the soft mud created by a rainstorm the evening before. In the hot sun, the mud and prints dried and hardened and were buried by other layers of mud containing still more dinosaur prints.

Over the centuries, the buried layers and prints would turn to rock such as shale. Erosion and earthquakes eventually brought some of the footprint-bearing

Dinosaur print in rock

rocks back to the surface, allowing a geologist to crack apart the layers to reveal the tracks, like someone turning the pages of a photo album.

From about 200 to 190 million years ago, conditions in southeastern New York, near Nyack, were just right for creating fossilized tracks. As the African continent struggled to pull apart from North America, a deep valley formed there, called by geologists the Newark Basin, a false start for the eventual separation that would create the Atlantic Ocean. The valley filled with mud, and dinosaurs left their footprints before the mud hardened.

However, that era was in the early part of the age of dinosaurs, before the larger and better known of their breed, such as tyrannosaurus rex, had developed. So the footprints that have been found in the Newark Basin are from a relatively small Triassic Period dinosaur, about the size of a large ostrich, called coelophysis.

Dinosaurs became extinct about 65 million years ago after a massive meteor struck the earth. It's believed that so much dust was blasted into the atmosphere, where it lingered for years, that the climate cooled dramatically, killing off much of the earth's vegetation. Larger animals, such as dinosaurs, that required great amounts of vegetation or that fed on animals that did, could not survive.

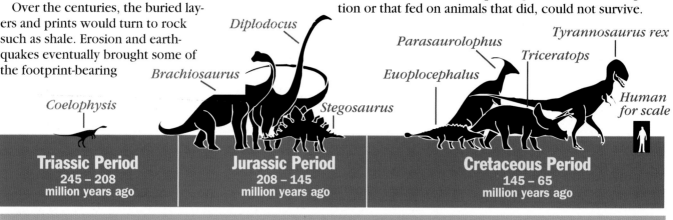

Diplodocus
Brachiosaurus
Coelophysis
Stegosaurus
Parasaurolophus
Euoplocephalus
Triceratops
Tyrannosaurus rex
Human for scale

Triassic Period
245 – 208
million years ago

Jurassic Period
208 – 145
million years ago

Cretaceous Period
145 – 65
million years ago

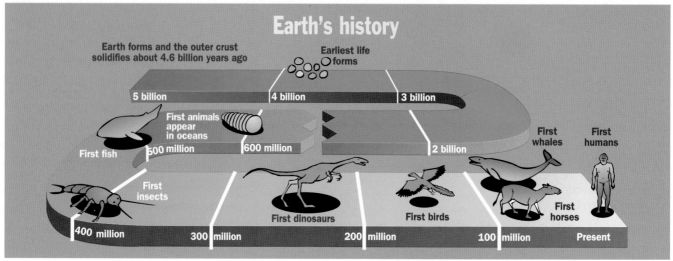

Earth's history

Earth forms and the outer crust solidifies about 4.6 billion years ago

Earliest life forms

5 billion

4 billion

3 billion

First animals appear in oceans

First fish

500 million

600 million

2 billion

First whales

First humans

First insects

400 million

300 million

200 million

100 million

Present

First dinosaurs

First birds

First horses

Taughannock Falls, Trumansburg

It was the dead of winter even in the heart of summer. It was the ice age.

During the last two million years, there have been four major advances of continental glaciers into the northern United States from centers in Canada.

The most recent ice age began about 70,000 years ago when a glacier that had formed in eastern Canada slowly expanded, eventually covering most of the Northeast. In some places, the ice was more than a mile thick. The glacier, called by geologists the Laurentide ice sheet, also spread west, covering most of Canada and the northernmost United States from the Rocky Mountains eastward. It did not begin to melt away from the Northeast until 21,000 to 22,000 years ago.

Glaciers form when the climate of a region cools enough so that snow builds up in winter faster than it melts in summer. Just as a snowball turns to an ice ball if you squeeze it hard enough, snow, if it continues to pile up, can eventually become so compressed that much of it turns to ice, especially at the bottom of the pile.

The increase in snow and ice year in and year out can create a mound of ice so high that the weight of it causes the ice to begin to spread slowly outward at the bottom, like thick maple syrup flowing on a tabletop, except at a much slower pace. A glacier may advance at a speed of only a few feet a year, or it may travel hundreds of feet a year.

Even at this relatively slow speed, though, a glacier can move a great distance over thousands of years, as it did during the last ice age.

Much of the landscape of New York was shaped by the

North America's last ice age
Position of the ice about 21,500 years ago

Cordilleran ice sheet

Canada

Laurentide ice sheet

United States

glaciers that reached down into the Northeast. If there had been no glaciers, Long Island, the Great Lakes and the Finger Lakes would not appear as they do today.

A glacier can be like a bulldozer, widening and deepening valleys as it moves. Like a bulldozer, it may also push rocks and boulders along in front of it.

When the ice melts, the meltwater may fill the valleys it dug, forming lakes. And the debris that was pushed along at the front edge of the glacier may be left in a long pile called a moraine.

The beds of the Great Lakes and the Finger Lakes were ancient river valleys that were dramatically deepened by the action of glaciers. The land of Long Island was formed by glacial moraines and the sand, pebbles and other light debris carried by the flowing water from the melting ice.

The last glacier to cover New York stopped and began to melt back when it reached what is today the southern border of the state. Most of New York was not free of ice until about 11,000 years ago.

The glacial ice was filled with debris, and when it began to melt, the heavier material in it was simply dropped to the ground. New York, like much of the Northeast, shows the evidence of this. The soil is filled with glacially rounded stones. Large boulders, called erratics, are also scattered across the landscape.

However, once the ice was gone from an area, the landscape did not immediately spring back to life. It was probably frozen, barren and blanketed with snow much of the year, a wasteland covered with rocks and other glacial debris. Low tundra vegetation, similar to what you would see near the Arctic today, grew on it for centuries.

The first human beings arriving in the Northeast after the last ice age may have encountered very cold conditions indeed.

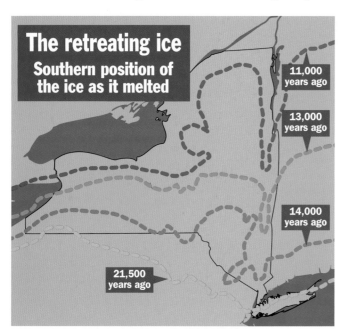

The retreating ice
Southern position of the ice as it melted

11,000 years ago

13,000 years ago

14,000 years ago

21,500 years ago

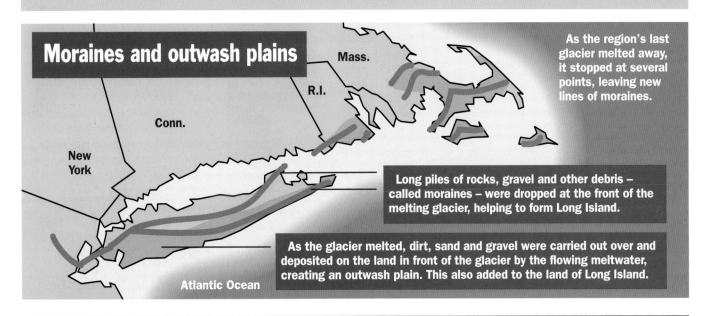

Moraines and outwash plains

Mass.

R.I.

Conn.

New York

As the region's last glacier melted away, it stopped at several points, leaving new lines of moraines.

Long piles of rocks, gravel and other debris – called moraines – were dropped at the front of the melting glacier, helping to form Long Island.

As the glacier melted, dirt, sand and gravel were carried out over and deposited on the land in front of the glacier by the flowing meltwater, creating an outwash plain. This also added to the land of Long Island.

Atlantic Ocean

Animals of the Ice Age

Giant cats with teeth like daggers. Shaggy-coated, long-tusked creatures that looked like elephants. Beavers larger than a man. Bison weighing a ton and a half. Musk oxen, ground sloths, wild pigs and caribou.

Some of the animals that roamed North America as the last ice age ended may have seemed to belong more to the age of dinosaurs.

The much colder climate of the northern parts of the continent 12,000 years ago provided a home to a different group of animals than one sees today, creatures that were able to survive on a frozen landscape.

However, as the ice melted away and the climate warmed, many of the same animals found in the Northeast today, including skunks, white-tailed deer, opossums, raccoons and black bears, also resided in the region.

It's believed the first humans arrived in North America between 11,000 and 12,000 years ago as the last ice age was ending. They may have hunted the largest of the ancient ice age animals to extinction in a matter of just 1,000 years, including the woolly mammoths and mastodons.

While bones of mammoths and mastodons have been found in New York, those of saber-toothed cats have not, although these fierce creatures are believed to have lived throughout North and South America.

Woolly mammoth
Height: 9 to 11 feet at the shoulder
Weight: 8,000 to 12,000 pounds

American mastodon
Height: 8 to 10 feet at the shoulder
Weight: 8,000 to 10,000 pounds

Saber-toothed cat
Length: 6 to 8 feet
Weight: 400 to 500 pounds

The first Americans may have been a small band of hunters traveling in search of caribou or woolly mammoths more than 11,000 years ago who had no idea they were about to discover a vast new continent.

During the last ice age, so much of the earth's water was still ice that the surface of the ocean may have been more than 300 feet lower than it is today. As a result, a temporary land bridge emerged connecting Asia to Alaska. Human beings had already spread through much of Europe, Africa and Asia, but North America was still uninhabited by people.

The earliest Americans may have entered Alaska and continued down through Canada, finding an open passage between the great sheets of ice that took them into the American Northwest. Living for so long in frozen conditions, they may have been startled as they continued to travel south and east and began to encounter warmer temperatures and the vast forests and fields of America's heartland.

Exactly when the first human beings arrived in North America is unclear. In the 1920s, stone arrowheads were

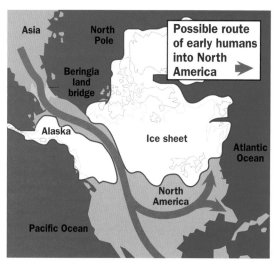

Possible route of early humans into North America →

found near Clovis, New Mexico, that date back about 11,500 years. Archaeological sites in Alaska have been found that date back 12,000 years.

The discovery of human settlements in South America that are about the same age suggests to some archaeologists that human beings may have entered Alaska 20,000 or even 30,000 years ago. However, others say humans could have moved much faster down the North American coast, especially if they traveled by ocean-going boats.

Nevertheless, the glacial ice did not begin to melt away from the Northeast until about 21,000 to 22,000 years ago, so humans did not enter this region until after that.

The first arrivals in North America, whom we now call "paleoindians," which means the oldest Indians, probably had lives many people today would envy. After all, many may have had a wealth of food, land to live on and leisure time.

Were they savages? Not at all, say anthropologists. They were just as intelligent and inventive as people today. Human beings have probably been thinking at our

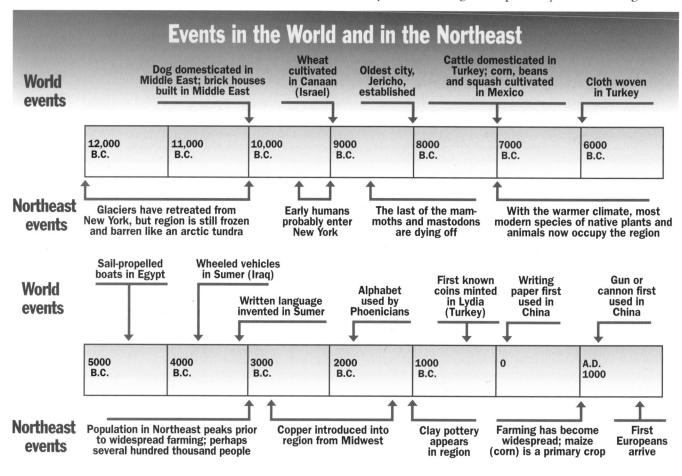

Events in the World and in the Northeast

		Dog domesticated in Middle East; brick houses built in Middle East	Wheat cultivated in Canaan (Israel)	Oldest city, Jericho, established	Cattle domesticated in Turkey; corn, beans and squash cultivated in Mexico	Cloth woven in Turkey
World events						
	12,000 B.C.	11,000 B.C.	10,000 B.C. 9000 B.C.	8000 B.C.	7000 B.C.	6000 B.C.
Northeast events	Glaciers have retreated from New York, but region is still frozen and barren like an arctic tundra		Early humans probably enter New York	The last of the mammoths and mastodons are dying off	With the warmer climate, most modern species of native plants and animals now occupy the region	

	Sail-propelled boats in Egypt	Wheeled vehicles in Sumer (Iraq)	Written language invented in Sumer	Alphabet used by Phoenicians	First known coins minted in Lydia (Turkey)	Writing paper first used in China	Gun or cannon first used in China
World events							
	5000 B.C.	4000 B.C.	3000 B.C.	2000 B.C.	1000 B.C.	0	A.D. 1000
Northeast events	Population in Northeast peaks prior to widespread farming; perhaps several hundred thousand people		Copper introduced into region from Midwest		Clay pottery appears in region	Farming has become widespread; maize (corn) is a primary crop	First Europeans arrive

First humans in New York

Archaeologists are detectives, piecing together clues about ancient people from the things they left behind. Occasionally, they find tools, artwork, trash or the remains of the buildings of the earliest residents of the Northeast. However, these artifacts have often been scattered, broken or changed through the centuries, making it difficult to determine what the earliest people in the region were like or how they lived.

Humans probably entered what is today New York between 11,000 and 11,500 years ago. In Athens in Greene County, a site called West Athens Hill by archaeologists appears to have been a quarry used by early humans for perhaps thousands of years to mine chert, a type of rock also called flint, that was used to make points for tools and weapons.

Sites with high-quality chert were rare in the Northeast, and chert from the Hudson River Valley has been found in much of New England, indicating that West Athens Hill may have been a place widely known to the earliest inhabitants of the Northeast.

Recreation of paleoindians gathered at the West Athens Hill site (Courtesy of the New York State Museum)

modern level of complexity for the past 50,000 years. That means there was just as much genius among these early people as there is among modern humans. There was also just as much greed, charity, cruelty and compassion then as now.

It's true that life for humans has changed dramatically over the centuries as their inventions and discoveries have accumulated. But their basic emotional and intellectual makeup has changed very little. If these early human cultures did not advance much beyond the use of simple tools, it's because there was little need for them to advance. By many standards, they were "rich" people. Their needs could be easily met. Indeed, they may have enjoyed life as much, if not more, than most people today.

Paleoindians were a people frequently on the move, following the migration paths of the herd animals, such as caribou, or the waterfowl, such as ducks and geese, that they hunted. They also fished and trapped small game animals, such as beavers and rabbits, and they gathered and ate fruits, berries, nuts and some plants. In fact, plant matter may have made up much of their diet.

They probably carried their limited belongings on sleds or toboggans drawn by domesticated dogs or pulled by

members of the group. Their tools included hammers, chisels, axes and awls (hole makers) made from rock, as well as other implements, such as sewing needles, made from bones or the ivory of mammoth tusks.

The sewing needle dates back at least 40,000 years. So the first Americans probably wore tailored clothes of furs and skins. And they probably lived in tents made of skins that had been loosely sewn together.

They would camp, possibly for weeks or months at a time, near where animals were known to seek food or water, for instance by a river, near a forest opening or around ponds or marshes. They would eventually move on, but if the hunting, fishing and berry picking were good enough, they might return to the same spot the next season.

The earliest residents of the Northeast probably had rich spiritual and social lives. Studies of modern-day hunting and gathering societies, such as those discovered in tropical rain forests, show they can be masters of conversation. Without television and books, talk is their main source of entertainment and information.

They also relied on speech to pass along the knowledge accumulated over thousands of years – effective herbal cures, tips for hunting game, and designs of tents or layouts of camps.

It is likely they passed their abundant leisure time doing craftwork, playing with wooden toys or games, singing and dancing, and just absorbing the beautiful scenery.

As the number of people grew in a region, it is also likely that many families came together at certain times of the year for festivals where goods were traded, stories swapped and marriages arranged.

Certainly, medicine was not as advanced as it is today. But the simplicity of that era offered its own protection. The level of stress was probably very low. With so much food and land, war was probably not yet common, although personal arguments and hostilities have always existed.

While more babies died in infancy than die today, those who survived childhood could often live into their forties or fifties. American Indians did not suffer many of the medical problems that are now widespread, such as obesity, diabetes and high blood pressure, which often result from inactive lives and diets high in fat.

Indeed, when the first Europeans arrived in America, they were struck by the great health American Indians seemed to enjoy.

What was life like for the American Indians of the Northeast? Four centuries ago, before Europeans settled widely in the region, life was simple in many respects and it was cyclical. It had the seasons as its clock.

Many American Indian families would live by the seashore or a riverbank in summer, to fish and to farm. In winter, those by the coast might move to protected inland areas to hunt squirrels, beavers, deer, moose or bears and to live off stored supplies of vegetables, nuts and berries.

Farming became common in the Northeast about 1,000 years ago. By A.D. 1600, crops included maize (corn), beans, squash, pumpkins, cucumbers and tobacco.

In upstate New York, five tribal groups banded together, perhaps as early as A.D. 1500, for mutual protection and greater collective strength. Known as the Iroquois Confederacy, the original five were the Mohawks, who lived in the Mohawk River Valley, and the Senecas, Cayugas, Onondagas and Oneidas, who lived in central and western New York.

The Iroquois people often lived in farming villages made up of several longhouses surrounded by high wooden fences. Longhouses might be 50 to 200 feet long, 20 feet high and 20 feet wide. They were construct-

Crafting points for tools and weapons

American Indians hunted game animals with spears and arrows and cleaned them with knives. The points on these tools and weapons were often made from rock called chert or flint. When chert was tapped with a sharp rock or other hard tool, flat flakes would come loose, allowing the rock to be fashioned into the desired shape.

Paleoindians would chisel grooves, called flutes, into the sides of the points so that once the point was finished, it might be tightly inserted into a notch in a stick. It was then tied into place with animal tendons, leather strips or other stringy material.

Points were sometimes made from other types of rock, including obsidian and quartzite.

Fluted points found in New York
(Courtesy of the New York State Museum)

*Recreation of paleoindian
shaping chert*

Recreation of Iroquois constructing longhouses
(Courtesy of the New York State Museum)

ed from frameworks of wooden poles that were covered with bark.

The fences were made of long poles stuck in the ground. They served as protection in time of war, but they also kept out animals, such as wolves, and were a barrier against winter winds.

Inside a large longhouse, 15 to 20 families might live, each with its own section of the open interior. Fires would be spaced throughout the structure, with smoke escaping through holes in the ceiling. Each fire was shared by two families,

Longhouses could be smoky and noisy, with children and dogs scampering about. In summer, people would sleep or sit on raised wooden platforms. In winter, they might sleep on woven reed mats laid by the fires, perhaps with blankets of animal furs.

Food, such as corn or smoked fish, would be stored in large wooden tubs or casks. Valuable personal items might be placed in ceramic jars and then buried in the ground beneath sleeping areas. Other items might be placed on shelves above the sleeping platforms.

The Iroquois Confederacy was headed by a Grand Council made up of sachems who were elected by the women in each tribe. If they weren't doing a good job, sachems could be voted out of office.

To create open spaces for farming and for foot paths, American Indians of the Northeast might periodically burn over the land, destroying the underbrush and many of the trees. The practice would also create more open land for hunting, and it would kill off insect pests near villages.

Throughout the Northeast, American Indian women were responsible for raising children, preparing meals and tending the crops and the home. Men were hunters, warriors and craftsmen, making the tools, utensils and weapons needed for survival.

American Indian children, especially boys, were encouraged at a young age to be bold and self-reliant. To prove he had reached manhood, a young male might be led blindfolded into the woods in winter, armed with a bow and arrow, a knife and a hatchet, and be expected to survive on his own until spring.

The most common clothing for both men and women in warm weather was the breech clout, a belt and cloth that performed the same function as a pair of shorts does today. In colder weather, sewn layers of animal skins might be worn, often of raccoon or fox, with the fur side of the skin against the body.

When the first Europeans arrived in the region in the early 1600s, there may have been several hundred thousand American Indians living in the Northeast.

However, diseases contracted from the earliest European trappers and traders – smallpox, measles, influenza, typhoid fever and tuberculosis – killed many American Indians. They had no history of these new illnesses and little or no immunity to them.

The first epidemic of the European illnesses, believed to include smallpox, probably began in 1615. By the late 1630s, up to 95 percent of the American Indians in some areas of the Northeast had died from the diseases.

Because of disease and wars with Europeans, by 1800 the American Indian way of life, which had defined how humans lived in the region for nearly 100 centuries, had disappeared from much of the Northeast.

Some of the world's most magnificent mountains were once found in the Northeast. The Taconic Mountains along New York's eastern border once rivaled any peaks in the world today in height.

But that was hundreds of millions of years ago. All those years of rain and wind, and the freeze and thaw of water in their crevices, have steadily eroded these peaks. Today, the region's mountains are minor when compared with mountains in other parts of the world.

The high peaks of New York are concentrated in two regions – the Adirondack and Catskill mountains. Much of southeastern New York is a coastal plain along the Atlantic Ocean. Much of western New York is rolling hills and plains, land that gradually slopes to the Great Lakes.

The highest point on Long Island, Jayne's Hill in Suffolk County, is only 401 feet above sea level. In western New York, the highest point is Alma Hill in Allegany County. Its peak is 2,548 feet above sea level, less than half the height of New York's tallest peak, Mount Marcy in the Adirondacks.

The Adirondacks are often described as new mountains made of old rock. It's believed that heat deeper in the earth has been pushing a dome-shaped region of rock into the air over the past 20 million years, forming the Adirondacks. Erosion has created the separate peaks and valleys. However, the peaks, which are made of rocks more than a billion years old, continue to rise about 10 inches a century.

The Catskills, a region of lower but still impressive peaks to the south, formed in a different manner than the

View of Whiteface Mountain in Wilmington in the Adirondacks

Adirondacks. Some 350 to 380 million years ago, magnificent mountains in New England eroded, and great amounts of sediment were washed by rivers into New York, settling in a shallow inland sea that covered much of the state.

That thick layer of sediment eventually hardened into rock, and where most of the sediment settled in eastern New York, it became the raw material for the Catskills.

How the Adirondacks formed

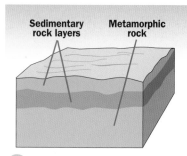

1 Before the uprise began perhaps 20 million years ago, older, tougher metamorphic rock lay beneath layers of newer, softer sedimentary rock in a region that was largely a flat plain.

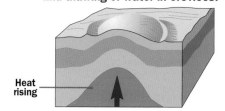

2 Heat rising from deeper within the earth gradually pushed up a dome. The softer sedimentary rock on the surface began to erode from wind, rain and the freezing and thawing of water in crevices.

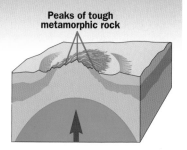

3 Today, much of the sedimentary rock on the surface has been lost to erosion. The tougher metamorphic rock beneath, which has resisted erosion, continues to rise and now makes up the peaks of the Adirondack Mountains.

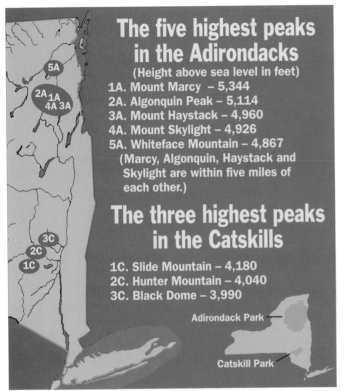

The five highest peaks in the Adirondacks
(Height above sea level in feet)

1A. Mount Marcy – 5,344
2A. Algonquin Peak – 5,114
3A. Mount Haystack – 4,960
4A. Mount Skylight – 4,926
5A. Whiteface Mountain – 4,867
(Marcy, Algonquin, Haystack and Skylight are within five miles of each other.)

The three highest peaks in the Catskills

1C. Slide Mountain – 4,180
2C. Hunter Mountain – 4,040
3C. Black Dome – 3,990

Adirondack Park

Catskill Park

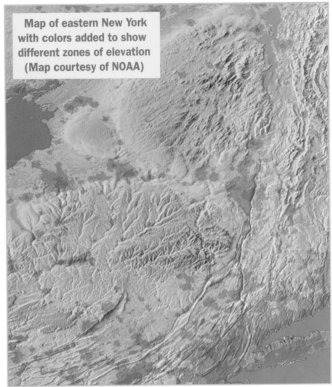

Map of eastern New York with colors added to show different zones of elevation (Map courtesy of NOAA)

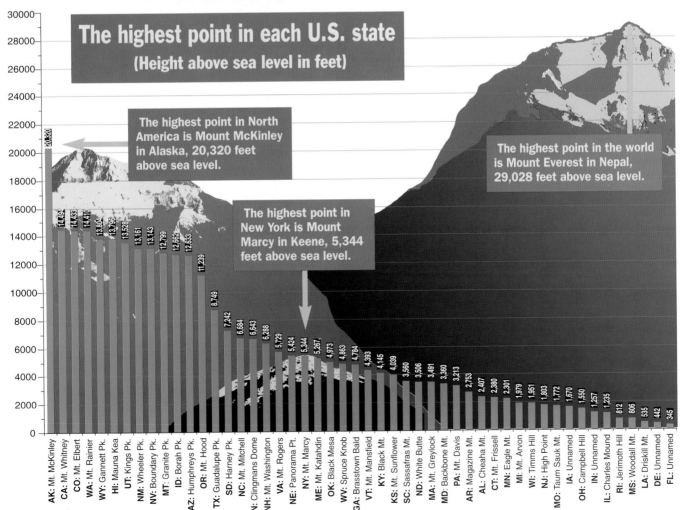

The highest point in each U.S. state
(Height above sea level in feet)

The highest point in North America is Mount McKinley in Alaska, 20,320 feet above sea level.

The highest point in the world is Mount Everest in Nepal, 29,028 feet above sea level.

The highest point in New York is Mount Marcy in Keene, 5,344 feet above sea level.

State	Height
AK: Mt. McKinley	20,320
CA: Mt. Whitney	14,494
CO: Mt. Elbert	14,433
WA: Mt. Rainier	14,410
WY: Gannett Pk.	13,804
HI: Mauna Kea	13,796
UT: Kings Pk.	13,528
NM: Wheeler Pk.	13,161
NV: Boundary Pk.	13,143
MT: Granite Pk.	12,799
ID: Borah Pk.	12,662
AZ: Humphreys Pk.	12,633
OR: Mt. Hood	11,239
TX: Guadalupe Pk.	8,749
SD: Harney Pk.	7,242
NC: Mt. Mitchell	6,684
TN: Clingmans Dome	6,643
NH: Mt. Washington	6,288
VA: Mt. Rogers	5,729
NE: Panorama Pt.	5,424
NY: Mt. Marcy	5,344
ME: Mt. Katahdin	5,267
OK: Black Mesa	4,973
WV: Spruce Knob	4,863
GA: Brasstown Bald	4,784
VT: Mt. Mansfield	4,393
KY: Black Mt.	4,145
KS: Mt. Sunflower	4,039
SC: Sassafras Mt.	3,560
ND: White Butte	3,506
MA: Mt. Greylock	3,491
MD: Backbone Mt.	3,360
PA: Mt. Davis	3,213
AR: Magazine Mt.	2,753
AL: Cheaha Mt.	2,407
CT: Mt. Frissell	2,380
MN: Eagle Mt.	2,301
MI: Mt. Arvon	1,979
WI: Timms Hill	1,951
NJ: High Point	1,803
MO: Taum Sauk Mt.	1,772
IA: Unnamed	1,670
OH: Campbell Hill	1,550
IN: Unnamed	1,257
IL: Charles Mound	1,235
RI: Jerimoth Hill	812
MS: Woodall Mt.	806
LA: Driskill Mt.	535
DE: Unnamed	442
FL: Unnamed	345

Lily pads on a pond

When the Erie Canal opened in 1825, connecting Albany to Buffalo and the Hudson River to the Great Lakes, it created a much-needed waterway from the Atlantic Ocean to the Midwest through New York state. And it immediately made New York City the most important port on the East Coast.

All along this inland water route, though, cities grew and industrial pollution spoiled local rivers and lakes. In the 1960s, Lake Erie was pronounced dead from pollution, and in the Hudson River and many other New York rivers, raw sewage could be seen floating in the current.

However, with the passage of the federal Clean Water Act in 1972, and with citizen and government action to clean up the state's waterways, many became clean enough that today they are recreational attractions instead of places to be avoided.

With New York's 7,800 lakes and ponds and 52,000 miles of rivers and streams, there is no shortage of water in the state. And that doesn't include the Great Lakes and Atlantic Ocean on its shores.

The presence of so much water produces a great diversity of wildlife. There is a long list of plants and animals that live only in water, and another long list of wildlife that live alongside water.

The land surface of New York generally slopes toward the Great Lakes and St. Lawrence River in the north and toward the Atlantic Ocean elsewhere in the state. These gradual slopes have produced one group of rivers that flow generally north, such as the Genesee, Oswego and Black rivers, and another set that flow generally south or southeast, such as the Hudson and Delaware rivers.

Most New Yorkers get their water from municipal reservoirs or from wells that tap underground lakes of water, called aquifers, places where water collects beneath the surface but doesn't drain away.

The 9 million people who live in New York City and Westchester County use nearly 1.2 billion gallons a day of water drawn from a series of reservoirs north of the city.

The main water supply in Syracuse is Skaneateles Lake. Residents of Rochester and Long Island get their water from municipal wells that tap aquifers.

Most communities in the state receive 32 to 48 inches of precipitation a year, an amount that helps to keep these water supplies full.

The Atlantic shore

Lake or pond?

The usual definition of a pond is that it is shallow enough for aquatic plants to grow anywhere in it. But a lake can be so deep and dark in places that plants only grow in the shallow areas.

Wetlands

Between dry land and the deep water of lakes, rivers or the ocean, you will often see wetlands, areas where land and water mix, such as swamps, marshes, bogs, wet meadows and riverbank forests that may flood after heavy rains.

Wetlands were once considered places of no value in much of America, and in the last two centuries more than half the acreage of wetlands in the lower 48 states has been filled, drained or otherwise lost.

But wetlands do have great value, people have learned. They filter out pollution before it reaches larger bodies of water, and they are home to many kinds of plants and animals, from cattails to muskrats, that are seen almost nowhere else. That's why wetlands are now protected by law.

Since 1780 in New York, nearly 60 percent of the state's wetlands have disappeared, most of them inland freshwater wetlands. The state now has about a million acres of freshwater and saltwater wetlands.

Muskrat

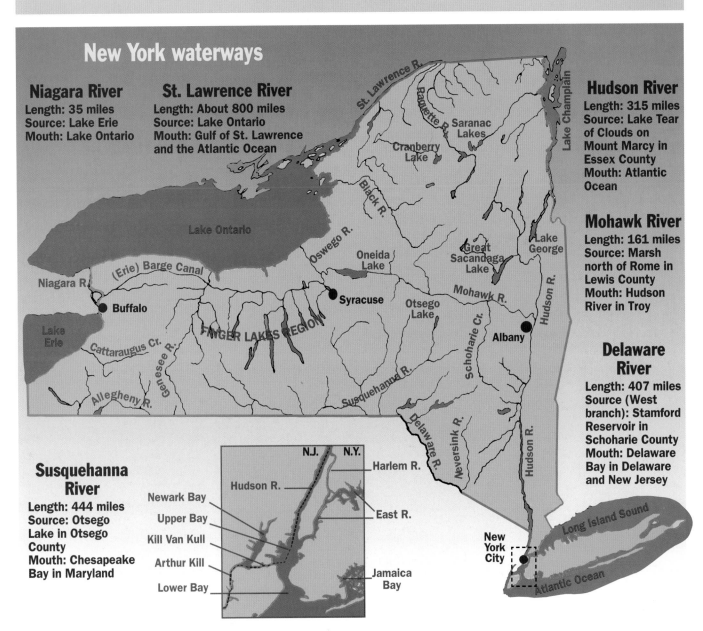

New York waterways

Niagara River

Length: 35 miles
Source: Lake Erie
Mouth: Lake Ontario

St. Lawrence River

Length: About 800 miles
Source: Lake Ontario
Mouth: Gulf of St. Lawrence and the Atlantic Ocean

Hudson River

Length: 315 miles
Source: Lake Tear of Clouds on Mount Marcy in Essex County
Mouth: Atlantic Ocean

Mohawk River

Length: 161 miles
Source: Marsh north of Rome in Lewis County
Mouth: Hudson River in Troy

Delaware River

Length: 407 miles
Source (West branch): Stamford Reservoir in Schoharie County
Mouth: Delaware Bay in Delaware and New Jersey

Susquehanna River

Length: 444 miles
Source: Otsego Lake in Otsego County
Mouth: Chesapeake Bay in Maryland

The Finger Lakes

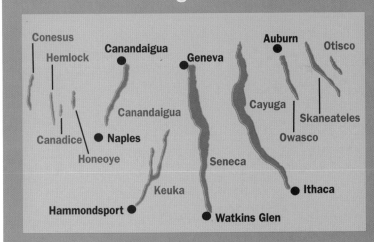

The Finger Lakes were formed by glacial action during past ice ages. Streams probably carved out the initial valleys of the lakes, but then advancing ice deepened them dramatically. Rocks and other debris dropped by ice after it melted eventually dammed the valleys to the south, and the meltwater from the retreating ice during the most recent ice age filled the lakes.

Today, all the Finger Lakes drain north into Lake Ontario.

Seneca Lake, the largest of the lakes by volume, is 38 miles long and 3 miles across at its widest point. It has a maximum depth of 618 feet, and it can hold 4.2 trillion gallons of water.

Cayuga Lake is the longest of the lakes. It is 40 miles long, has a maximum depth of 435 feet, and can hold 2.5 trillion gallons of water.

The Great Lakes

The Great Lakes, when combined, are the largest body of fresh water in the world, covering an area of 94,000 square miles, nearly twice the area of New York state.

Like the Finger Lakes, the Great Lakes were formed during recent ice ages when a series of advancing glaciers carved the lake basins. As the last glacier retreated about 12,000 years ago, the water from the melting ice filled the five massive lake beds.

Only Lake Michigan is entirely within U.S. borders. The other four lakes are shared with Canada. The lakes are connected together by rivers, straits and canals. The water flows from west to east, emptying into the St. Lawrence River and then into the Atlantic Ocean.

The Great Lakes system is so large that it may take more than two centuries for a drop of rain falling into Lake Superior to flow all the way to the ocean.

The smallest of the lakes by volume, Lake Erie is only 210 feet deep at its deepest point, and it may freeze over in winter. By contrast, Lake Superior, the largest of the

lakes and the largest freshwater lake in the world, reaches 1,333 feet in depth and normally does not freeze over.

An easy way to remember the names of the Great Lakes is to remember the word "homes" – Huron, Ontario, Michigan, Erie and Superior.

The American Falls at Niagara Falls

Niagara Falls

Waterfalls often form where an area of hard rock meets an area of soft rock in a place along a river with rushing water. The soft rock erodes but the hard rock does not, leaving sharp drops in the river's path.

Along the Niagara River, which links Lake Erie to Lake Ontario, hard dolostone and limestone can be found with more easily eroded sandstone and shale, and the result is one of the most spectacular falls in the world, Niagara Falls.

However, the falls are a traveling show. The rock layers over which the water tumbles have gradually eroded so that the falls may now be 7 miles upstream from where they were 12,000 years ago.

The falls used to move an average of 3 feet per year upstream until water was diverted in the 1950s to create electricity and to stabilize the erosion. Now less water is sent over the falls during certain times of the year, and the water is spread more evenly over the crest lines. The falls currently erode at a rate of about an inch per year.

There are two main waterfalls at Niagara Falls – the Canadian Falls, where the water falls about 170 feet, and

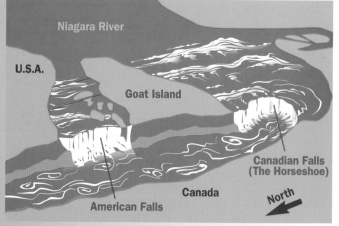

the American Falls, where the water drops from 70 to 110 feet onto piles of rocks below. The actual height of the American Falls is about 180 feet.

The Canadian Falls is also known as the Horseshoe because of its shape.

During the summer months, nearly 45 million gallons of water may flow over Niagara Falls each minute.

Spuytenduival Stream in the Pharoah Lake Wilderness Area in Horicon

Normal daily temperature (°F)

January maximum

- 40°-45°
- 35°-40°
- 30°-35°
- 25°-30°
- 20°-25°

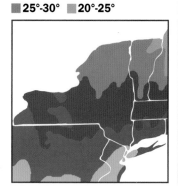

January minimum

- 25°-30°
- 20°-25°
- 15°-20°
- 10°-15°
- 5°-10°
- 0°-5°

July maximum

- 85°-90°
- 80°-85°
- 75°-80°
- 70°-75°

July minimum

- 65°-70°
- 60°-65°
- 55°-60°
- 50°-55°
- 45°-50°

Local measurements may differ sharply depending on such things as elevation, position in relation to mountains or large water bodies, and the urbanization of the area.

Annual snowfall

- 12 - 24 in.
- 24 - 36 in.
- 36 - 60 in.
- 60 - 100 in.
- 100+ in.

Peak colors of fall foliage

- Sept. 20 - Oct. 1
- Sept. 25 - Oct. 5
- Oct. 1 - Oct. 12
- Oct. 3 - Oct. 15
- Oct. 5 - Oct. 18
- Oct. 12 - Oct. 25
- Oct. 15 - Oct. 29
- Oct. 23 - Nov. 5

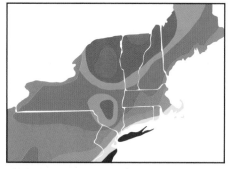

Annual precipitation

- 24 - 32 in.
- 32 - 40 in.
- 40 - 48 in.
- 48 - 56 in.

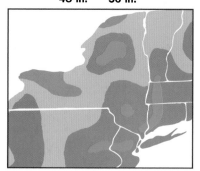

Sunrise and sunset in New York

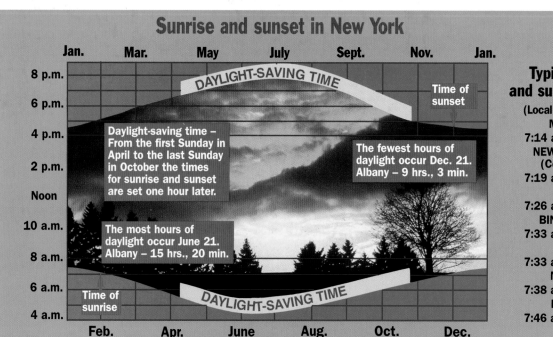

Daylight-saving time – From the first Sunday in April to the last Sunday in October the times for sunrise and sunset are set one hour later.

The most hours of daylight occur June 21. Albany – 15 hrs., 20 min.

The fewest hours of daylight occur Dec. 21. Albany – 9 hrs., 3 min.

Time of sunrise

Time of sunset

DAYLIGHT-SAVING TIME

Typical sunrise and sunset for Jan. 1
(Local adjustment - EST)
MONTAUK
7:14 a.m. 4:32 p.m.
NEW YORK CITY
(Central Park)
7:19 a.m. 4:39 p.m.
ALBANY
7:26 a.m. 4:32 p.m.
BINGHAMTON
7:33 a.m. 4:43 p.m.
UTICA
7:33 a.m. 4:37 p.m.
MASSENA
7:38 a.m. 4:29 p.m.
BUFFALO
7:46 a.m. 4:51 p.m.

New York	Jan.	Feb.	Mar.	Apr.	May	June	July	Aug.	Sept.	Oct.	Nov.	Dec.	Total or annual avg.
Snowfall (inches)	7.5	8.5	5.1	0.9	T	0	0	0	0	T	0.9	5.5	28.4
Precipitation (inches)	3.42	3.27	4.08	4.20	4.42	3.67	4.35	4.01	3.89	3.56	4.47	3.91	47.25
Normal daily max. temp.	37.6	40.3	50.0	61.2	71.7	80.1	85.2	83.7	76.2	65.3	54.0	42.5	62.3
Normal daily min. temp.	25.3	26.9	34.8	43.8	53.7	63.0	68.4	67.3	60.1	49.7	41.1	30.7	47.1
Clear days (avg.)*	8	8	9	8	8	8	8	9	11	12	9	9	107
Cloudy days (avg.)**	14	11	12	12	11	10	10	10	9	9	12	13	133

Albany	Jan.	Feb.	Mar.	Apr.	May	June	July	Aug.	Sept.	Oct.	Nov.	Dec.	Total or annual avg.
Snowfall (inches)	16.8	13.9	11.4	2.7	0.1	T	T	0	T	0.2	4.2	14.4	63.7
Precipitation (inches)	2.36	2.27	2.93	2.99	3.41	3.62	3.18	3.47	2.95	2.83	3.23	2.93	36.17
Normal daily max. temp.	30.2	33.2	44.0	57.5	69.7	79.0	84.0	81.4	73.2	61.8	48.7	34.9	58.1
Normal daily min. temp.	11.0	13.8	24.5	35.1	45.4	54.6	59.6	57.8	49.4	38.6	30.7	18.2	36.6
Clear days (avg.)*	5	6	6	5	5	5	6	7	8	8	4	5	70
Cloudy days (avg.)**	18	15	17	16	16	13	12	13	12	14	18	19	183

Binghamton	Jan.	Feb.	Mar.	Apr.	May	June	July	Aug.	Sept.	Oct.	Nov.	Dec.	Total or annual avg.
Snowfall (inches)	20.3	17.4	14.6	5.0	0.3	T	0	0	T	0.7	7.4	18.0	83.7
Precipitation (inches)	2.40	2.33	2.82	3.13	3.36	3.60	3.50	3.36	3.32	2.89	3.28	3.00	36.99
Normal daily max. temp.	27.9	30.1	40.4	53.5	65.4	73.8	78.6	76.4	68.6	57.3	44.9	32.7	54.1
Normal daily min. temp.	14.3	15.3	24.7	35.2	46.2	54.6	59.7	57.9	50.6	40.3	31.6	20.3	37.6
Clear days (avg.)*	3	3	4	5	5	5	6	5	6	6	3	2	53
Cloudy days (avg.)**	22	19	20	18	17	14	13	14	14	17	21	23	212

Buffalo	Jan.	Feb.	Mar.	Apr.	May	June	July	Aug.	Sept.	Oct.	Nov.	Dec.	Total or annual avg.
Snowfall (inches)	24.3	17.8	12.0	3.2	0.2	T	T	T	T	0.3	11.6	23.1	92.5
Precipitation (inches)	2.70	2.31	2.68	2.87	3.14	3.55	3.08	4.17	3.49	3.09	3.83	3.67	38.58
Normal daily max. temp.	30.2	31.6	41.7	54.2	66.1	75.3	80.2	77.9	70.8	59.4	47.1	35.3	55.8
Normal daily min. temp.	17.0	17.4	25.9	36.2	47.0	56.5	61.9	60.1	53.0	42.7	33.9	22.9	39.5
Clear days (avg.)*	1	2	4	5	6	6	7	7	6	6	2	1	53
Cloudy days (avg.)**	24	20	19	17	16	12	11	12	14	16	23	24	208

* Average cloud cover 30% or less   ** Average cloud cover 70% or more   T = Trace of snow   (Source: NOAA)

The Natural History of New York

The authors would especially like to thank Alan Mapes of the New York Department of Environmental Conservation and George Hamell of the New York State Museum for their help in reviewing the material in this book.

Published by:
Hampshire House Publishing Company
8 Nonotuck St.
Florence, Mass. 01062
413-584-1706
www.hampshirehousepub.com

First printing – printed on recycled paper in the USA
Copyright © 2002 by Stan Freeman and Mike Nasuti
ISBN: 0-9636814-5-1
Library of Congress Control Number: 2002100160

Copy editors: Irmina Pulc, Barry Schatz and Julia Gaviria

Some of the material in this book is based on articles by the authors that originally appeared in the *Springfield Union-News and the Sunday Republican.*

Photography credits

All photos are by Stan Freeman unless otherwise noted. A photograph's position on a page is indicated as follows: T = top, C = center, B = bottom, R = right and L = left.

LANDSCAPES

Carl Heilman II (www.carlheilman.com) – 3, 56, 61
Bob McInnis (www.bobmcinnis.com) – 25
Joseph Melanson (www.skypic.com) – 43
Richard Welch (www.cayugaimages.com) – 49

GENERAL PHOTOGRAPHY

G. Francis Osborn (courtesy of Mildred Osborn) – 14T, 17R, 24CL, 26BCL, 29TR, 29B
For the U.S. Fish & Wildlife Service – Tom Stehn, 1BR; George Harrison, 34CR; Craig Koppie, front cover (falcon)
For NOAA – Ken Balcomb, 35L; Stan Butler, 35R
Corel – 9 (kestrel and red-tailed hawk), 10T, 10B, 11B, 14BCL, 16BL, 16BR, 60C

Red fox

This series highlights the natural history of individual states. We began with a basic book, essentially a collection of articles, and we are attempting to adapt it to each state in the series. So some material in this book, including text, illustrations and photographs, is repeated from book to book in the series.

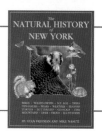